"Books on spiritual warfare, Harold Ristau tells us, are 'a dime a dozen.' And most aren't worth even that paltry price. This gem is a happy exception. Far from the shock-and-awe demonic encounters many of us have come to expect, what Ristau delivers is christologically rooted, biblically minded, and traditionally rich. It is a pastorally sound treatment of the workings of the unseen realm of angels and demons. Remember pastor, you 'fight from within the fortress of Christ's office and hide behind his person.' For that one sentence, you ought to buy this book. And there's lots more where that came from!"

—Tim Perry,
dean, Providence Theological Seminary

"Harold Ristau covers a lot of territory in the small compass of his newest book: angelic ministry, dealing with the demonic and exorcism, the necessity of forgiveness, the priestly work of pastors. Though compact, it is rich with spiritual insight and wisdom, especially for Western Christians, far too many of whom have embraced the circumscribed reality of their secular neighbors. It is a tremendous spur to pondering and meditation, confession and thanksgiving, and living our daily lives in simple reliance on the invincible power of God."

—Michael A. G. Haykin,
chair and professor of church history,
The Southern Baptist Theological Seminary

"Since pastors are rightly skeptical about the current fascination with demons and angels in popular culture, they find it hard to deal with the increasing number of people who find it much easier to believe in demons and angels than in the living God, people who fancy that they possess themselves and own their bodies and yet fear that they may be possessed and owned by these dark powers. In this eloquent guidebook on spiritual care, which is both modest in its claims and wide ranging in its scope, Harold Ristau introduces them to the hidden dimension of their work as a spiritual contest together with Jesus and the angels against the evil spirits and the devil. He does not provide pastors with a handbook on exorcism, which would, of course, be only of limited use, but shows how the ministry of deliverance permeates all that they do and are. His focus is not mainly on deliverance from demons but on the delivery of people from the domain of darkness by Jesus through the forgiveness of sins and the ministry of the gospel in the service of worship and in pastoral care. Drawing on the Scriptures as God's word, the wisdom of the church, and his own pastoral experience, he equips them to discern the works of the devil clearly in the church and the world and encourages them to counter his ways confidently with the resources that Christ himself supplies."

—John W. Kleinig,
emeritus lecturer, Australian Lutheran College,
Adelaide; author *Wonderfully Made:
A Protestant Theology of the Body*

Spiritual Warfare

For the Care of Souls

LEXHAM MINISTRY GUIDES

Spiritual Warfare

For the Care of Souls

HAROLD RISTAU

General Editor
Harold L. Senkbeil

LEXHAM PRESS

Spiritual Warfare: For the Care of Souls
Lexham Ministry Guides

Copyright 2022 Harold Ristau

Lexham Press, 1313 Commercial St., Bellingham, WA 98225
LexhamPress.com

Print ISBN 9781683596219
Digital ISBN 9781683596226
Library of Congress Control Number 2022933928

Lexham Editorial: Todd Hains, Abigail Stocker, Danielle Thevenaz
Cover Design: Joshua Hunt, Brittany Schrock
Typesetting: Abigail Stocker

*Dedicated to my mother and father
who carried me into the kingdom of God,
for which I am forever grateful.*

Contents

Acts 20:28

Pay careful attention to yourselves and
to all the flock, in which the Holy Spirit
has made you overseers, to care
for the church of God,
which he obtained
with his own
blood.

Series Preface

Wʜᴀᴛ'ꜱ ᴏʟᴅ ɪꜱ ɴᴇᴡ ᴀɢᴀɪɴ.

The church in ages past has focused her mission through every changing era on one unchanging, Spirit-given task: the care of souls in Jesus' name. Christian clergy in every generation have devoted themselves to bringing Christ's gifts of forgiveness, life, and salvation to people by first bringing them to faith and then keeping them in the faith all life long.

These people—these blood-bought souls—are cared for just as a doctor cares for bodies. The first step is carefully observing the symptoms of distress, then diagnosing the ailment behind these symptoms. Only after careful observation and informed diagnosis can a physician of souls proceed—treating not the symptoms, but the underlying disease.

Attention and intention are essential for quality pastoral care. Pastors first attentively listen with Christ's ears and then intentionally speak with Christ's mouth. Soul care is a ministry of the word; it is rooted in the conviction that God's word is efficacious—it does what it says (Isa 55:10–11).

This careful, care-filled pastoral work is more art than science. It's the practical wisdom of theology, rooted in focused study of God's word and informed by the example of generations past. It's an aptitude more than a skillset, developed through years of ministry experience and ongoing conversation with colleagues.

The challenges of our turbulent era are driving conscientious evangelists and pastors to return to the soul care tradition to find effective tools for contemporary ministry. (I describe this in depth in my book *The Care of Souls: Cultivating a Pastor's Heart.*) It's this collegial conversation that each author in this series engages—speaking from their own knowledge and experience. We want to learn from each other's insights to enrich the soul care tradition. How can we best address contemporary challenges with the timeless treasures of the word of God?

IN THE LEXHAM MINISTRY GUIDES YOU WILL meet new colleagues to enlarge and enrich your unique ministry to better serve the Savior's sheep and lambs with confidence. These men and women are in touch with people in different subcultures and settings, where they are daily engaged in learning the practical wisdom of the care of souls in real-life ministry settings just like yours. They will share their own personal insights and approaches to one of the myriad aspects of contemporary ministry.

Though their methods vary, they flow from one common conviction: all pastoral work is rooted in a pastoral habitus, or disposition. What every pastor does day after day is an expression of who the pastor is as a servant of Christ and a steward of God's mysteries (1 Cor 4:1).

Although the authors may come from theological traditions different than yours, you will find a wealth of strategies and tactics for practical ministry you can apply, informed by your own confession of the faith once delivered to the saints (Jude 1:3).

OUR LORD DOESN'T CALL US TO SUCCESS, AS IF the results were up to us: "Neither he who plants nor he who waters is anything, but only God who gives the growth" (1 Cor 3:7). No, our Lord asks us to be faithful laborers in the service of souls he has purchased with his own blood (Acts 20:28).

Nor does our Lord expect us to have all the answers: "I will give you a mouth and wisdom" (Luke 21:15). Jesus, the eternal Word of the Father, is the Answer who gives us words when we need them to give to our neighbors when they need them. After all, Jesus sees deeper into our hearts than we do; he knows what we need. He is the Wisdom of God in every generation (1 Cor 1:24).

But wisdom takes time. The Lord our God creates, redeems, and sanctifies merely by his words. He could give us success and answers now, but he usually doesn't. We learn over time through challenges and frustrations—even Jesus grew over time (Luke 2:52). The Lexham Ministry Guides offer practical wisdom for the church.

MY PRAYER IS THAT YOU GROW IN HUMBLE appreciation of the rare honor and responsibility that Christ Jesus bestowed on you in the power and presence of his Spirit: "As the Father has sent me, even so I am sending you" (John 20:21).

Father in heaven, as in every generation you send forth laborers to do your work and equip them by your word, so we pray that in this our time you will continue to send forth your Spirit by that word. Equip your servants with everything good that they may do your will, working in them that which is well pleasing in your sight. Through Jesus Christ our Lord. Amen.

Harold L. Senkbeil, General Editor
September 14, 2020
Holy Cross Day

Prayer for the Ministry of the Word

Since the earliest days of the church, Christians have used holy Scripture to shape and inform their life of prayer. The structured prayer below invites pastors and laity to celebrate God's victory over sin, Satan, death, and hell, and invoke our Triune God's help in the spiritual warfare in which his church daily engages. It can be used by either individuals or groups—in which case a designated leader begins and others speak the words in bold font.

☩

In the name of the Father, Son, and Holy Spirit.
Amen.

O Lord, open my lips,
And my mouth will declare your praise.   *Ps 51:15*

He who dwells in the shelter of the Most High
> **will abide in the shadow of the Almighty.**

For he will deliver you
> from the snare of the fowler
> **and from the deadly pestilence.**

He will cover you with his pinions,
> and under his wings you will find refuge;
> **his faithfulness is a shield and buckler.**

Because you have made the Lord
> your dwelling place—
> **the Most High, who is my refuge—**

no evil shall be allowed to befall you,
> **no plague come near your tent.**

For he will command his angels concerning you
> **to guard you in all your ways.**

On their hands they will bear you up,
> **lest you strike your foot**
> **against a stone.**   *Ps 91:1, 3–4, 9–12*

Let us pray.

That he would equip and empower his faithful
> saints with the gifts of his spiritual armor, the
> service of his holy hosts, and the weapon of
> his mighty word,

That they may rest secure in the gracious promises received in his church as they fight the good fight of the faith in prayer and in praise.

That they would boldly confess the truth and devote themselves with zeal to the mission of rescuing the lost from the domain of darkness and transferring them to the kingdom of God's beloved Son.

Lord, in your mercy,
Hear our prayer.

That God would send his powerful, healing and comforting Spirit upon all pastors of Christian congregations.

That he would arm them for the great and difficult tasks set before them as they are strengthened by the blood of the Lamb.

That he would protect them from all temptations of body and soul in their angelic ministry to his people.

Lord, in your mercy,
Hear our prayer.

Our Father who art in heaven
Hallowed be thy name,
Thy kingdom come,
Thy will be done on earth as it is in heaven;
Give us this day our daily bread;
And forgive us our trespasses as we forgive
    those who trespass against us;
And lead us not into temptation,
But deliver us from evil.
For thine is the kingdom, and the power, and
    the glory for ever and ever.
Amen.   *Matt 6:9–13*

Almighty and merciful God, our Heavenly Father, you sent forth your only Son and his holy angels to defeat the powers of Satan. You continue to pierce the darkness through the forgiveness of sins and the light of your church. Send your Holy Spirit to shield and deliver your holy people from the perils of misbelief, despair, shame, and vice. Preserve your flock from all evil by faithful shepherds who care for their souls. Grant wisdom, humility, and courage as they minister to your people who worship you in the midst of the entire company of heaven.

Through Jesus Christ, your Son, our Lord, who lives and reigns with you and the Holy Spirit, one God, now and forever.

Amen.

The Lord bless us, protect us from all evil, and bring us to everlasting life.

Amen.

CHAPTER 1

Send Your Holy Angels

Guide us waking, O Lord, and guard us sleeping,
that awake we may watch with Christ and
asleep we may rest in peace.
—*Compline Antiphon*

BOOKS ON SPIRITUAL WARFARE ARE A DIME A dozen. It's a popular topic because every faithful Christian is assaulted by the unceasing attacks of the world and the devil in his or her day-to-day life. The shelves of my local Christian bookstore are cluttered with self-help material listing ways to subdue temptation and prevent the evil one from gaining territory. Fictional novels on the subject compel us to question whether God is actually in control of the universe and if he could use our help. A few books address the unique spiritual and

mental struggles that pastors suffer in their ministries. Then there are the rarer, more intriguing
books on demon possession. These books can feel
like the snuff of Christian literature for both clergy
and laity alike; when we read them to satisfy curi-
osity, they can make our spiritual lives even worse.

The one book that stands out amidst this
jumble—the Holy Bible—offers us the only entirely
trustworthy window into these unseen realities,
ensuring that we're not "outwitted by Satan" (2 Cor
2:11) through ignorance or misunderstanding.
When we peer through the glass of God's word,
we see that "the light shines in the darkness, and
the darkness has not overcome it" (John 1:5). We
find ourselves surrounded by demons but also an
army of angels, supporting and caring for us in our
ministry. And every divine warning and threat is
followed by words of peace and promise for repentant believers.

This book helps prepare pastors as they devote
their lives to equipping the saints to battle our
common foe (Eph 4:12). For when it comes to
questions around the subject of spiritual warfare,
what you see isn't necessarily what you get. Looks
can be deceiving, especially since the great deceiver
disguises himself as an angel of light (2 Cor 11:14). If

we could see with our eyes what we know with our hearts—that our enemies aim their arrows incessantly—we would value our ministries more and show greater care in the ways in which we conduct them. After all, Satan's mission is to prevent your people from getting to heaven. He does it by distracting you from defending yourself, protecting your people, and using your God-given armor. Pastors fight the good fight of faith and empower others to do the same (1 Tim 6:12). They clothe their sheep when they preach "sound doctrine" (Titus 2:1) without compromise. They nourish their sheep by leading them in God-pleasing worship (Ps 29:2). They uplift them as living sacrifices by inspiring them to remain "holy and acceptable to God" (Rom 12:1).

At the end of the day, at the end of their lives, and at the end of the world, the job of the shepherd is to get his lambs into the sheep pen of heaven.

GUIDING SHEEP TO HEAVEN

"Precious in the sight of the LORD is the death of his saints" (Ps 116:15). Let's not let our joy become overshadowed by the tears and grief at a Christian funeral. Another soul for whom our Redeemer shed his blood has passed into the kingdom of glory. Alleluia! Another guest at the heavenly banquet has arrived, even as all Christians—both the living and the dead—await the final resurrection. Praise the Lord! That pastor can rest in peace celebrating the fact that, as a spiritual warrior, he has once again foiled the enemy's hellish plans. The apostolic ministry has triumphed, as it always does; a whole string of shepherds, through whom our Chief Shepherd worked, were likely instrumental in the victory.

Every pastor knows that it is dangerous to live by sight, for the victory remains hidden in the form of a cross. Yet we pastors forget how significant our calling is. Because the choices that people make in their short time on earth have repercussions for their eternal destinies, your job is one of the most important in the world. So, although the world thinks you are just performing empty ceremonies and ancient rituals that are therapeutic at best, God sees it differently.

The pastoral ministry is indispensable to the salvation and preservation of souls. And yet, if you are a sinner, you screw things up. God knows us better than we know ourselves—both our strengths and weaknesses. And so God doesn't let us go at this important task alone. He gives us help and helpers: the angels outnumber the demons at least three to one, so we have no reason to fear (Rev 12:4; 1 John 4:18). Even though this "host of heaven" (1 Kgs 22:19) has been worshiping the Triune God since their creation, their top priority since the fall of humankind is serving us. God sends angels to assist us in resisting our temptations and to strengthen us in both body and soul in our trials.

Two Kinds of Holy Angels

Just as you have angels, you may be surprised to hear that you too are an angel to others. You may have never thought about your vocation in this way. You are called as a messenger of the word. In fact, a synonym for the Hebrew word for "angel" is "messenger." These ambassadors of God are sent as preachers to us. And just as the identity of angels is inseparable from their office, it is the same with pastors.

Angels are like pastors in some unexpected ways. Both are sent to help others in need. By far the best aid available to humankind is the proclamation of the saving gospel to disheartened sinners with a message like "Do not be afraid" (Matt 28:5). We find the angels announcing Jesus' conception

(Luke 1:31), the birth of John, who would prepare the way for Jesus (Luke 1:13), the birth of Jesus (Luke 2:10–12), the guardianship of Jesus (Matt 1:20; 2:13, 19), and the resurrection of Jesus (Luke 24:23). In addition, most biblical scholars would argue that the Old Testament "angel of the Lord" is the preincarnate eternal Christ (Judg 13:18). Though we don't know for sure, it is an appropriate title for the Word who would become flesh and dwell among us (John 1:14).

After all, Jesus is both the message and the messenger. So his servants—both human and celestial—are dedicated to delivering Jesus into the ears, lives, hearts, and souls of people in word and deed.

One obvious difference between clergy and angels is that the angelic race is older than the human one. Because their population is complete, they don't need to get married (Matt 22:30). This society of bodiless creatures were created during creation, like us. But because death is, by definition, the separation of body and soul, they never die (Rom 6:23). Besides, they are sinless, perfect, and holy. They were, in effect, *born* divine messengers. In contrast, pastors are *formed into* messengers. They undergo study and training and, of course, receive a divine call. Yet despite these differences, together with angels, pastors are created and sent by God as ministers of mercy to his precious people. And despite your sins, imperfections, unholiness, and inadequacies, God confidently assigns a small flock to your care.

Celestial Reinforcement

He does it with the help of angels. Ministers need the celestial angels' ministry as much as anyone else. They come to the rescue of God's people in their dire times of need—and so do you.

As remarkable as it may sound, what they do for you, you do for others. As you are sent to serve others, angels are unceasingly being sent to serve you. Is there any greater comfort than the assurance that you aren't alone in your ministry? God governs and watches over the universe through the agency of the angels, which includes you!

In your common mission, serving your common Lord, don't be surprised when you find yourself in their company. Angels and pastors have a common love for worship. Christian worship offers an incomparable consolation in those moments when we feel like we are islands unto ourselves. Repeating our forefathers' sacred practices with their enduring resonance reminds us that the Lord's army is larger than a few clusters of Christian soldiers. Recollecting that the words with which we strengthen our people weren't created by us but come "from the mouth of God" (Matt 4:4) keeps us humble. We worship in a massive company of not only angels but all those who have fallen asleep in the Lord. Acknowledging both the tininess of our personhood and the timelessness of our message, the words are also a safeguard when we are tempted to minister to "our" people as lone rangers or one-of-a-kind spiritual heroes.

Delivering People from Hell

Some pastors and seminary professors teach that demons don't pester people in a Western, first-world context like ours. It's not true. Yet even when the invisible war manifests itself in strange and disturbing physical ways, we don't need to be frightened. As a retired military chaplain with an unusual amount of experience in the spheres of mental health, demonic oppression, and even possession, I hope to give you tools—some elementary, some specific to those in a pastoral vocation.

This book isn't intended to offer a crash course in angelology and demonology. Instead it unpacks pastoral applications of what we confess in the Nicene Creed—that God created "all things visible and invisible," and for his good and sovereign will. The message is a simple one: when God calls us to ministry, he makes sure that we are good to go. He gives us the necessary weapons, instruments, and tools—namely, his holy word and sacraments. His gifts suffice to equip us for whatever challenges await us in pastoral ministry. And we will even find that sometimes, our worst enemy—the devil—is used by God for spiritual edification and the advancement of his kingdom. He too may have a role to play.

God's grace and power never cease to surprise us. For, as St. Paul writes, "the weapons of our warfare are not of the flesh but have divine power to destroy strongholds" (2 Cor 10:4). Praise God that his holy word supersedes all of our human reasoning and self-imposed expectations. For the care of souls, we've already got all that we need.

Chapter 2

The Church Is Bigger than *Your* Church

Let your light scatter the darkness,
and illumine your Church.
—Versicle for Evening Prayer

OUR CHURCHES SURE FEEL SMALL IN THE grand scheme of things. That's true whether you pastor a church in an urban setting, overshadowed by skyscrapers, or a rural one, dwarfed by endless wheatfields. The world suggests that we are rather insignificant. From a human perspective, the unbeliever is right. They see a lonesome man with a white collar, carrying a beat-up Bible under his arm. But from heaven's perspective, you are a messenger of almighty God, and the church is bigger than your congregation.

The Bible describes the church not as a bunch of individual communities tied together with some common interests but as one single body founded upon the one confession of faith in Jesus as Lord. It is a huge population of both the living and the dead. In this unique community, all are saints "washed ... in the blood of the lamb" (Rev 7:14). The saints in heaven aren't worried about the future. They don't agonize about numbers. They just worship. They simply enjoy each other's company. We gather with them from our earthly dwellings. It's a mystery. We don't hear them, but we join them in their triumphant song daily. Like turning on your radio, you join a song that is already playing and that continues after you switch it off. Every time we "worship in spirit and truth" (John 4:24), we tap into that ongoing song. We don't see them, but "surrounded by so great a cloud of witnesses" (Heb 12:1), they cheer us on in our race of faith. The book of Revelation tells us that together with the angels, the saints in heaven worship and pray at "the golden altar before the throne" (Rev 8:3). Our prayers on earth are intermingled with theirs in heaven as one holy and apostolic church.

This population of holy servants includes the powerful army of angels. If the Lord were to reveal

to us the vast multitude of angelic armies that surround us—innumerable holy ones—like he did to
the prophet Elisha, we would behold an encouraging "mountain ... full of horses and chariots of
fire" (2 Kgs 6:17). Yet not everyone rejoices in their
magnificent glory and might.

FIERY DARTS

Unfortunately, where God builds a church, the
devil builds a chapel. The fallen angels are close
too. They seek to discourage us and distract us
from the truth, tempting us to believe the Lord's
army is small and his ministers don't matter. They
constantly whisper lies in our hearts. They often
heckle us through the voices of the secular and
unbelieving world.

When I served an inner-city congregation in
Montreal, many unchurched people were openly
critical of our church's mission and its values, in
spite of all the social services we also provided to
refugees and immigrants. I encountered countless
government agents who were entirely oblivious to
the holistic help that we sought to provide, caring
for people's temporal and eternal needs. They
were awestruck by my claim that the most chal-
lenging work involved spiritual concerns and not

bodily ones. Some would smirk when discovering the intense preparation that most clergy undergo: "How hard can ministry be? Why would you need a university degree?"

We might be told we're imperialist or judgmental when we try to convert people to our religion. The more antagonism toward the Christian worldview, the louder these voices sound. When Christians become progressively convinced by "every lofty opinion" (2 Cor 10:5), in spite of our best efforts to debunk them, we become frustrated and angered by the spiritually deafening noise.

Instead, Jesus tells us to pray, "Deliver us from the evil one" (Matt 6:13 NIV). Our sense of alienation and defeat can only be addressed by faith in the fact that God's kingdom "is not of this world" (John 18:36). The ways of the world pose no threat to the King of Glory, who has "overcome the world" (John 16:33).

REMEMBERING THE MISSION

When Christians forget that the church is bigger than they think, and that their mission is governed by the Holy Spirit and does not depend on their power, they behave as if their congregation is the only one in God's kingdom. With this mindset, success and advancement of the gospel depends upon their efforts alone. Even the toughest, most faithful ministers are bound to shatter under such pressure.

Stories of disillusioned congregations who have aimed high, believed strongly, and hoped greatly that their pastor is "the one" are common. They want a savior—a tangible and visible god in whom they can put their trust. In this scenario, no one can measure up. We see it in the employee contracts, call documents, or search committees: they want to hire someone who is youthful but also wise with age. He needs to have a lot of kids but also lots of time. Congregations want a faithful teacher but also a nice guy who avoids offending people. The list goes on.

Pastors don't help when they try hard to measure up to the unrealistic expectations placed upon them by others or themselves. Most pastors are attracted to the ministry because they want to make people's lives better. They want to serve because they love. Yet they soon discover that their salary depends on the satisfaction of their members. They feel like they are being rated, and if they haven't performed well enough, their "customers" may go somewhere else. Meanwhile they pray and truly want the best. The feeling of isolation deepens. Regardless of whether you have other clergy around, on a team or in town, it's still lonely in the day to day.

A perfect pastor doesn't exist, even in the most ideal circumstances. There is only one God, and we are not him! Those who seek perfection on earth have underestimated the sinful nature and idolized temporal things. Clergy need to remember that without the intervention of the Lord and his angels, they can easily forfeit the eternal prize, "lest after preaching to others I myself should be disqualified" (1 Cor 9:27).

Although pastors do their best to practice their angelic ministry, they end up usurping the place of Jesus Christ.

So God does a couple of things to make sure we don't ruin ourselves through self-righteous behavior or despairing attitudes. He forces us to accept that the battle involves more than one. Just as every army is made up of many soldiers, with different roles and skill sets, so too God's church includes a vast array of warriors. "If all were a single member, where would the body be?" (1 Cor 12:19). He teaches us how to surrender our unhealthy independence and depend on him—by getting us to rely on other Christians. And he makes us rely on our angelic friends.

THE SUPPORT OF THE SAINTS

God has generously offered all the gifts and talents that are needed for true Christ-centered ministry, but they are not all found in one person or even one congregation (Eph 4:16). His distribution decisions make sure that we reach out to each other for help and support. Some overly independent-minded pastors think too highly of themselves. Others are suspicious or jealous of others. This all amounts to distrust of God's design for the church; "woe to him who is alone when he falls and has not another to lift him up!" (Eccl 4:10).

In God's world, we are stronger together than apart. A chord with many strands is not quickly broken (Eccl 4:12). Nobody is good at everything. Wise pastors notice and appreciate the talents of others so that they can help to put them to the best use. When pastors pretend that they have all the gifts, they are set up for failure. The wisest pastors create opportunities for their people to use their talents and gifts instead of assuming that they are the only ones that can do the job. It not only saves time but honors the diversity God created in his church. Spiritual warfare is best conducted as a team.

The congregation needs the pastor, who has a unique role to play in the church family, and the pastor needs the congregation. They go hand in hand. "Iron sharpens iron, and one man sharpens another" (Prov 27:17). We are not self-sufficient. The devil would have us believe the opposite. And "if a house is divided against itself, that house will not be able to stand" (Mark 3:25).

ONE FOUNDATION

Jesus alone, as God, is entirely autonomous, yet he chooses to include us in his holy family, Trinitarian community, and divine fellowship. Although he is self-sufficient and has no intrinsic need of others, he decides to "need" them, inasmuch as a head needs a body in order to be complete. So he becomes the head of the body, the one universal and apostolic church, for which he gave his life. The fact that he is One, and that we are all individual members of his one mystical body, precludes self-fulfilling individualism, egoistic self-reliance, and independent beliefs. Accordingly, there is only one celebration of the Lord's Supper in time and space, although it happens repeatedly

in congregations of all times and all places. True
family fellowship and communal love is expressed
in a common confession of faith at God's one altar
as Christians are gathered together from all the
ends of the earth.

We shouldn't lament our inadequate, broken,
and suffering communities. Instead, we praise God
for them. Again and again they force us to look
outside ourselves to Jesus, for help and meaning.
And in Jesus, we don't find a motivational speaker
or flashy preacher. Rather, we encounter a beaten,
bloodied, and powerless Jewish criminal fastened
to a stick in the ground.

At Calvary, our eyes also behold a true picture
of ourselves and the fatality of sin. But when we
let that vision move us toward a reality beyond
that which meets the naked eye, we discover that
not only does crucifixion mean forgiveness, but it
means that our individual and communal identity
is grounded in the resurrection promise.

So we find that we are already victorious: kings
and queens, soldiers, and heroes, in that same Man
of Sorrows—a single sacrifice for sins (Heb 10:12)—
and in his body dwelling on earth: the church. We
have been sanctified through the "offering of the
body of Jesus Christ once for all" (Heb 10:10).

Through faith, we see our church through a new lens. Our empty churches are filled with saints and angels. Our crippled congregations are considered precious stones in the walls of a heavenly cathedral. Our shattered lives are revealed in perfect health. Jesus promised his disciples that they would see greater things than the miracles that they witnessed (John 1:50). I believe that these are some of them.

The Struggle to See by Faith

Unfortunately for us temporally sighted individuals, the one holy and apostolic church doesn't *look* like a strong, healthy, and victorious community. When my members complain about the hard-to-get-along-with people in their church—the least "comely parts" (1 Cor 12:24 KJV)— I remind them that in church we not only receive God's love, but we also learn to love each other. After all, we will be living together with one another for eternity. For, from our perspective, the body of Christ, the church, often looks like a prostitute. But from God's perspective, he sees a glorious virgin bride.

We heap coals on the head of the devil when we respond to the difficult people in our congregations and lives with love. After all, "we do not wrestle against flesh and blood, but against the rulers, against the authorities, against the cosmic powers over this present darkness, against the spiritual forces of evil in the heavenly places" (Eph 6:12). Spiritual war is fought with love.

Dealing with difficult members provides learning opportunities—chances to grow and mature in our pastoral ministry. That doesn't mean pastors can't be firm or that they need to embrace a form of positive thinking that denies sin, ignores evil, or reaches inside themselves, looking for tools to help effect improvement. Rather, we should serve with hope, "remembering before our God and Father your work of faith and labor of love and steadfastness of hope in our Lord Jesus Christ" (1 Thess 1:3). And even when things aren't happy, when they look bleak, we serve with joy, even though we may not feel joyful. Jesus summarizes the ministry as washing other's feet (John 13:1–17). Though it's always a dirty affair, it is good. Even amidst sorrow, pastors are "always rejoicing" (2 Cor 6:10). Yes, we are sinners, but we can minister with our chins held high, knowing we are forgiven and Christ is victor. When we don't, we aren't the only ones who suffer. So does our flock.

Healthy Spiritual Leaders

Even if they may not say it, our parishioners can tell when we are in poor spiritual and mental health. Lack of self-awareness hinders targeted repentance. Consequently, our ministry is exposed to new spiritual attacks.

The character and attitude of the leader sets the behavior of the community. Pastors lead their flocks. The laity imitate them (Heb 13:7). For better or for worse, the pastor's character cultivates the shape of the community. Pastor should take warning, since the standard is higher for them and they will "have to give an account" for the decisions they have made as they watch over souls (Heb 13:17). Certainly God still works through neglectful pastors—and in us all, in spite of our sin. He is gracious, and he won't let our sins get in the way of his ultimate goals. Yet we ought not put him to the test. Rather, we strive to be as spiritually, emotionally, mentally, and physically healthy as possible.

We Christians try our best to embody and reflect the heavenly country to which we journey, with the birth certificate we received in our conversion by faith and baptism. Certainly as sinners, our experience resembles that of refugees in a foreign land. But we are citizens of heaven, royal children of the King. We are temples of the Holy Spirit, though we may often feel like or appear as abandoned, derelict shacks.

Our personal and congregational lives are filled with temptation and turmoil. Pastors do their best to counter these sights and feelings by comforting Christians with the truth. The truth changes lives. People tend to live up or down to the expectations that you set for them. I learned this well when I spent a little time as a volunteer in prison chaplaincy. If you treat a criminal like an animal in a cage, he will behave like a threatened beast. If you treat him with some dignity, there is a better chance that he will amend his ways. He is more likely to begin acting in a way befitting of his status in the human race.

When Christians learn that they are saints by grace through faith alone, not because of something they have done or can do but due to Christ's declaration from the cross and tomb, they will be more inclined to live like the saints that they are. They are already citizens of heaven (Phil 3:20). They simply need to be reminded. My homiletics professor once wisely said, "Sanctification is descriptive rather than prescriptive. It's something that happens to you rather than something you do. Our people need to be encouraged to be what they are." Telling them to be better doesn't make them so. Proclaiming Jesus, and their new identity in him, does.

Even though good works do not save, when pastors embrace holy living, they help refute the idea that heaven is a distant reality with little bearing on our everyday lives. Observing virtuous Christian lives may not cause others to believe more, but it will certainly help slay all efforts to believe less. We are not saved by the example of the saints, but we are inspired by them. When we acknowledge the truth of our God-given identity and repent daily of our unholy lives that don't match up, we wrestle from the devil one of his most dangerous weapons in his menacing attacks on our Christian communities: doubting God's word of promise.

Just as angels were both carriers of a holy message and also embodied holiness in their very nature, pastors are the ambassadors of God in both word and deed. Paul isn't arrogant when he says, "Imitate me, just as I also imitate Christ" (1 Cor 11:1

NKJV). Our people naturally imitate their leaders, for better or for worse.

And as much as pastors have wished that they could have a private life, it's not likely. Just as a parent isn't able to really get a lot of "me time" away from the family and the kids, a pastor's personal life is intimately tied to the life of his flock. Your spiritual health and any other priorities you set have direct consequences on those whom you lead.

Self-care, then, is not selfish. To the contrary, your spiritual health matters to your congregation. We tell our people that they are not alone in whatever struggles they endure: physical, psychological, spiritual. We tell them that ministry is teamwork, and we are a body, and yet we often behave as if we are alone.

Some pastors may think that they don't need help. Yet it's not up to them, and that attitude is harmful to their neighbor. After all, unlike Buddhist communities, which consist of like-minded people who are perceived largely as islands unto themselves (with their highly individualistic piety of meditation), or Hinduism, which promotes a community governed by a shared fear (as worshipers are joined by one common interest, appeasing the vengeful gods through their sacrifices), or Islam, whose communities are largely unified by external factors (i.e., submission to rules by which to live), Christianity cultivates a deep and intimate spiritual interdependence between and amongst the faithful. It is the truest expression of community on earth. And after all, heaven is one massive divine community. Even the Holy Trinity is a divine community of three persons. God's kingdom includes more players and more diversity than we may expect. In short, there is no room for overly individualistic soldiers in the army of the Lord.

The Support of the Angels

Teamwork in the kingdom of God isn't just about leaning on other humans. It also means relying on others who are stronger and more holy than we: angels. This can be a humbling experience to the proud at heart or those who doubt that they are real. But it's a great comfort to those who believe the Bible at face value and already characterize ministry in terms of interdependence. When you're accustomed to partnering with your congregation, you'll also be more inclined to gladly accept the support of angels.

We couldn't have an honest or useful discussion of spiritual warfare unless we included the work of angels. *Honest,* because God made them, and they exist (Gen 1:31). *Useful,* because without them we would likely not survive spiritually. That is how crucial their work is as ministers of God: they are as important to the story of salvation as the biblical prophets and heroes of old. They are present at key events—announcing the births of John and Jesus and worshiping at the manger, preaching to soldiers and women at the empty tomb, encouraging the disciples at Christ's ascension into heaven. A "thousand thousands" serve God, and "ten thousand times ten thousand" stand before him (Dan 7:10), preparing to gloriously escort our Lord at his return. We even know some of their names: the archangel Michael (Rev 12:7) serves as commander of God's celestial armies and keeps Satan in his place. Gabriel (Dan 8:16; Luke 1:19, 26) functions as an appointed ambassador to humans, announcing the advent of our Lord to this world. They are powerful and mighty warriors: one angel put to death 185,000 of Sennacherib's army (2 Kgs 19:35). Just because we don't know the others' names doesn't mean that they aren't mighty or special in the sight of God.

When our God creatively designed the universe, including the multitude of holy angels, he made each one unique. And they've got jobs to do, just like everyone else in the kingdom of God. But they enjoy them, because they are perfect. They are holy.

These creatures of heaven have resided next to God since before the universe was completed, sharing in and reflecting his bright glory (Rev 18:1). They are both beautiful and awful—that is, full of awe. St. John writes, "Then I saw another mighty angel coming down from heaven, wrapped in a cloud, with a rainbow over his head, and his face was like the sun, and his legs like pillars of fire" (Rev 10:1). Due to their proximity to God and because they reflect his glory with their borrowed holiness, in virtually every biblical account where they appear to humans, angels cause people's hearts to tremble with terror, whether it was the prophets of the old covenant (Dan 10:8–19) or the shepherds in the new (Luke 2:1–12). They aren't our equals.

The marvelous host of angels is also an army, arranged accordingly. The Scriptures describe their ranks, which involves a hierarchy of thrones, dominions, principalities, and authorities (Col

1:16), including special kinds of angels called cherubim (Gen 3:24; Ps 80:1) and seraphim (Isa 6:2). Each company and every angel therin has a divinely assigned role in the orderly chain of command. Consider Gabriel, the Lord's unique messenger (Dan 8:16; Luke 1:19, 26). As God's appointed ambassador to humans, he has a special role in salvation history, announcing good tidings to biblical heroes and saints. Although our own histories are less significant in comparison, those same angels accompany us to announce the good news while protecting us with their powerful presence.

Angels are described as our guardians. When the conquest of Canaan was promised to the Israelites, God said, "Behold, I send an angel before you to guard you on the way and to bring you to the place that I have prepared" (Exod 23:20). They are called saviors: "In all their affliction he was afflicted, and the angel of his presence saved them; in his love and in his pity he redeemed them; he lifted them up and carried them all the days of old" (Isa 63:9).

Best of all, their powerful ministry doesn't stop with the canonization of Scripture. We have all heard stories of encounters with these heavenly creatures: one time, I barely avoided a serious car accident after a long road trip. It was as if something, or someone, had grabbed my steering wheel and saved me from a tragic disaster. I was relieved and puzzled. My vehicle seemed to have passed through another without a scratch! My mother remembers the appearance of a comforting and beautiful angelic presence at her bedside when she was a sick orphan in Lithuania during World War II. My father too recounts a miraculous escape from East Berlin in the 1950s when a communist soldier, after noticing that they possessed forged documentation, simply winked the family through the border control.

A skeptic could attribute these moments of salvation to good luck: a compassionate guard, mental delusion, or an overactive imagination due to extreme fatigue. Perhaps it makes little difference; for believers, God gets the glory. But if we could keep a record, the statistics would flash in our favor. Tradition holds that when Christians die, they need not fear the way to heaven, since their angels know the way. How many pastors have witnessed deathbed experiences where the dying one is fixated on an invisible entity in the room, followed by a peaceful expression and even a smile, before passing into eternity? "Can't you see them?" whispered an old man innocently as he fell asleep in the Lord. Side effect of morphine? I doubt it. Experienced pastors intuitively know the difference.

Most everyone I know has a story about angelic intervention in their lives. Again, catastrophes avoided are dismissed as coincidence instead of divine and angelic intervention. Yet I have also met many agnostics who are intrigued by the notion and will attribute such welcome, inexplicable events—like "miracles"—not to accident, but to divine intervention of some sort. God is at work amidst unbelievers as well.

This shouldn't surprise us. God even loves his enemies and provides daily bread to them too. The angels are active in people's lives everywhere. As countless as the myriad angels that Scripture depicts surrounding God's throne are the countless myriad of his miraculous holy acts.

ANGELS ASSIGNED TO YOU

You have an angel assigned to you—at least one (Matt 18:10). Each Christian has one. You probably got yours when you were baptized. They help us in our ministry, even though we aren't aware that they are there. When we're overwhelmed by the requirements of being a pastor, it's great to know that God supports you with the angels. Like Aaron holding up the arms of Moses, these servants of God lend you strength.

Let's be clear: cupids on Valentine's Day cards ought not to be equated with the Bible's holy and powerful angels. In fact, the cherubim aren't chubby flying babies but terrifying beings with flaming swords who maintain proper temple worship. They kept Adam and Eve out of Eden; the fruit of the tree of life was off-limits to sinners. No wonder we find images of cherubim in the temple, embroidered on the curtain and framing the mercy seat on the ark of covenant (Exod 25:20). You couldn't approach God without facing these holy and awesome security guards. They are characterized as powerful and mighty (Rev 18:1). When Jesus tells his disciples that he has more than twelve legions of angels at his disposal, he's talking about 72,000 of these divine warriors (Matt 26:53). Although no one knows their numbers, that is an impressive figure! A lot of angels! A lot of power! They demand our respect. The seraphim were not only holy but frightening, with their several sets of wings (Isa 6:2–6). These aren't creatures to mess with!

Yet they are on our side. The prophet Isaiah, overwhelmed by his unworthiness to preach the word, recounts how "one of the seraphim flew to me, having in his hand a burning coal that he had taken with tongs from the altar. And he touched my mouth and said: 'Behold, this has touched your lips; your guilt is taken away, and your sin atoned for' " (Isa 6:6–7). They anoint the lips and bless the words of all faithful preachers. And they don't just help you; your people also have angels assigned to them. Sometimes we forget that. Pastors are fathers of spiritual families. Parents' first priority is the welfare of their children—we are rightly protective. But sometimes we forget that God supersedes as Father over us. When we aren't available, or when we fail, his people are still safe and sound under his protection through his angels.

When we walk by sight, oblivious to these unseen helpers, we can become overly protective of our members. We forget in whose stead we serve—that we are ambassadors of Christ (2 Cor 5:20). Our sheep aren't actually ours. This is a great comfort. Our Over-Shepherd is mightier, wiser, and more competent than all of us under-shep-herds combined. He proves it by deploying his assistants to minister with us.

Angels don't just act on our behalf, they also appear among us incognito. It may only be in ret-rospect, after reflecting upon an unusual encounter with someone or something, that when you realize the facts didn't add up. You suspect an angelic man-ifestation. That mysterious person that helped you out earlier in the day, who seemed to just "appear out of nowhere"—perhaps an angel in human dis-guise. Some of the people to whom we have shown kindness or performed acts of charity may not have been who we thought. That's why we should "not neglect to show hospitality to strangers, for thereby some have entertained angels unawares" (Heb 13:2).

Disbelieving in what we can't see and what the world finds laughable doesn't hurt God; it only hurts us. Young children jump into the arms of their loving parents without any hesitation. As they age, they begin to doubt, even though their par-ents' commitment to them hasn't changed. Their lack of faith is to their own detriment. Doubt that God is gracious, kind, almighty, and involved in our daily affairs deprives us of his help, because we tend not to ask for nor expect it. If you believe a lie, you live accordingly. We become easy targets for the wicked angels' workings when we doubt the existence of demons, since it doesn't change their active involvement in our world. It only makes things easier for them!

The caricature of tails and horns are meant to distract us from taking demons seriously. And so we must "be sober-minded; be watchful. Your adversary the devil prowls around like a roaring lion, seeking someone to devour" (1 Pet 5:8). The devil's main strategy against us is to cause us to doubt God, dissuading us from being vulnerable children who rely solely upon their Father's care. When we opt not to acknowledge our sinful independence and self-sufficiency, God will find ways of getting us to depend on him—for our own good—through those humbling, unexpected crises in our Christian and parish lives.

Just consider the story of Gideon. His army was unnervingly outnumbered by the enemy (Judg 7:3–7)—and God still asks him to scale his forces back further, "lest Israel boast over me, saying, 'My own hand has saved me' " (Judg 7:2). Gideon is a mighty warrior—as his name suggests in the Hebrew—because of his faith, not because of his bodily might. Like Joshua before him, he let God fight the battle.

These biblical heroes trusted in God, not themselves. We all lack faith in God's might, and so we all need to repent for thinking the battle depends on our performance. Repentance, then, is not only *tolerating* the notion that we are weak and helpless, depending entirely upon God's goodness, but *celebrating* it. When we do, we don't just put up with the supposedly infantile idea of angels watching over us—we end up asking for them!

That's why, when I pray with my children at the beginning and end of the day, we say together: "Let your holy angel be with me, that the evil foe may have no power over me." As church father John Chrysostom said, "Near each one of us angels are sitting; and yet we snore through the whole night."[1] An eventide hymn puts it best: "They never rest nor sleep as we; / Their whole delight is but to be / With Thee, Lord Jesus, and to keep / Thy little flock, Thy lambs and sheep."[2]

ANGELS ARE OUR COMPANIONS

Believing in angels kills the sense of loneliness in ministry—especially when you feel fatigued and tired, a wounded warrior in a seemingly endless battle—by reminding us that we are surrounded by the great cloud of witnesses and heavenly saints (Heb 12:1). Frankly, if we believed ourselves to be surrounded by angels, our stress and anxiety levels would probably decrease.

Even if you belong to a church denomination or local ministerium that cultivates opportunities to gather with other pastors, it is rare to find yourself shoulder-to-shoulder with like-minded clergy. Monks in fraternal communities also struggle with feelings of depression, lamenting how others don't understand the challenges unique to their situation. Although your brothers in the ministry are family, they are also estranged, as the sinners we all are, on this side of heaven.

Yet, amidst the existential alienation that we feel in our ministries, we have the truest and most intimate family surrounding us at all times: God, the saints in heaven, and his holy angels. John Chrysostom remarks how magnificent it is that though "the space between angels and men is great; nevertheless [God] brings them down near to us, all but saying, For us they labor, for our sake they run to and fro: on us, as one might say, they wait on us. This is their ministry, for our sake to be sent every way."[3]

God's invisible helpers and warriors are at all times deployed to serve and protect those who will inherit salvation (Heb 1:14). They know our personal issues—spiritual and physical, and all the places where they overlap—and they do something about them. The angels are not just there observing what is going on. They are actively engaged in defending you from the enemy and guarding you from danger. The designated prayer (or "collect") for the Feast of St. Michael and All Angels reminds us of their deep-seated devotion to caring for us: "O everlasting God, who hast ordained and constituted the services of angels and men in a wonderful order: Mercifully grant that, as thy holy Angels always do thee service in heaven, so by thy appointment they may succour and defend us on earth; through Jesus Christ our Lord. Amen."[4]

For the angels are not only with us as a *community* of believers. Even better, our Lord Jesus Christ—true God and true man—is ever present with each *individual* member of his mystical body. As individuals and as the church, we exist as the temple of the Holy Spirit. Both God and angels are active. We belong to God, and he has invested his very life—the sweat and blood of his Son—into our wellbeing. "For we are God's fellow workers ... God's building" (1 Cor 3:9). Our Lord is not a crooked landlord who lets his property disintegrate with neglect. He cares for you.

Due to his intimate work in our lives, building his kingdom as we minister to his people, Jesus does not only sympathize with us pastors but "in every respect has been tempted as we are, yet without sin" (Heb 4:15). Jesus knows what it is like to be both human and a pastor. Jesus, according to his human nature, empathizes with us and our struggles. Yet there is great succor in the fact that, according to his divine nature, he is totally different from us. He is perfect, omniscient, and omnipotent. Fully aware of the deepest corners of our hearts and all dimensions of our situations, he has the power to help us in every personal and pastoral need. "Let us then with confidence draw near to the throne of grace, that we may receive mercy and find grace to help in time of need" (Heb 4:16).

That angels are not like us is a comfort, too. By virtue of their proximity to our Lord, they are holy, and the fact that they belong to the divine reality makes them not only more powerful than us but more useful in supporting us. Imagine having a business partner who was perfectly objective, devoted, and good. Your worries regarding the strength of your company would likely be reduced, wouldn't they? It's even better with angels, for they are holy.

Yet pastors and laity need to take care, lest we become too friendly with these magnificent creatures who support us. To see an angel in their splendor and glory—to gaze upon their holiness, to consider their power—right here and now would rightly terrify us. Whenever people encounter angels revealed in their splendor, they naturally fall on their faces in righteous fear, in light of their might and power. God's angels are known for shutting the mouths of lions (Dan 6:22), breaking open prison doors (Acts 5:19) and loosing a captive's chains (Acts 12:8), as if they were nothing, holding back the four winds of the earth (Rev 7:1), and wielding destructive power over the nations of the earth (Rev 18:21). They are able to help and save but, when appropriate, also destroy (Isa 37:36; Acts 12:23). Sometimes they come with righteous judgment, and other times with divine mercy. It's a lesson for us all, as we discern the best ways to apply God's word to the mixed-up lives of those whom we have been sent to serve.

Chapter 3

Angelic Ministry in a Demonic World

Stay with us, Lord, for it is evening,
and the day is almost over.
—Luke 24:29, *Versicle for Evening Prayer*

Pastoral ministry is compared with that of angels because we perform similar work and have similar authority. The Son of God appeared in order to destroy the devil's works (1 John 3:8). We take part in the destruction of unholy works when we pray in the Great Litany "that it may please thee to strengthen such as do stand; to comfort and help the weak-hearted; to raise up those who fall; and finally to beat down Satan under our feet. *We beseech thee to hear us, good Lord.*"[5] Authority to engage in this kind of spiritual warfare was given by Jesus to his first apostles (Matt 10:1) but is also extended to all faithful pastors today. This incredible truth can be overwhelming. You carry on in the apostolic office. *You* even cast out demons (Mark 3:15).

Healing the soul and exorcizing demons happen in more ways than you might imagine. The "ministry of deliverance" is distinguished from exorcism, specifically, since it involves more than rebuking demons—it includes all the ways in which pastors combat the vast array of demonic activity in Christians' lives. Although some believe that this ministry is a unique gift or specialized skill set given to only select Christians, I believe it is a function of the pastoral office and thus the responsibility of all pastors.

Each pastor has different natural abilities. Some find prayer easier than others. Some are better preachers, counselors, apologists, and so forth. Yet every pastor is involved in all of these activities to some degree. When your parishioner is admitted to the hospital, you visit, even though it may be out of your comfort zone. Though demon possession is rare, it happens, and when it does, pastors are compelled to respond. Whether or not you feel at ease practicing ministry in that specific environment, if one of your parishioners struggles with demon possession, it is your responsibility to address it. But for the most part, clergy deal more commonly with less dramatic demonic influences like demonic oppression, demonic attack, or manifestations common during certain points in Christians' lives, such as in times of intense temptation.

When it comes to demonic activity, a rule of thumb is this: when all mental health and medical possibilities are dismissed, then we can attribute the phenomenon to strictly spiritual factors. Popular culture and Christian media offer much misinformation about demons. But silly sensationalism doesn't undermine the reality of the devil and his work within the paranormal. I cannot overstate that pastors already practice a ministry of deliverance, delivering people from the clutches of the evil foe, whether they realize it or not. Every time there is a baptism, the devil is banished. Every time we practice faithful counseling, pastoral caregiving, teaching the word, and proclaiming the gospel, spiritual war is happening. Some of our parishioners' struggles are more acute and require specific weaponry. In all cases, angels are present, helping us.

THE WORK OF ANGELS TODAY

In the Bible, God surprises his people with angels. They appear at some of the most unexpected moments in ministry. When Jacob felt abandoned, they appeared to him in a dream: "the angels of God were ascending and descending" on a ladder reaching up to heaven from whence the Lord himself spoke (Gen 28:12). Ezekiel discovered new motivation to minister after receiving a vision of the cherubim in the temple (Ezek 10:1–20). Yet the roles of angels aren't limited to dreams and visions. Though bodiless, they are physically involved in our lives. They can act in material ways, such as the angels taking the hands of Lot, his wife, and his daughters to save them from destruction (Gen 19:15–16).

Borrowing divine might, they are sent to help God's people in times of trial, comfort them in crisis, or instruct them with a divine message, which the recipients may or may not want to hear. Sometimes they are deployed to carry out God's punishment on his enemies by pouring out the "bowls of the wrath of God" (Rev 16:1). Their work is always part of God's sovereign plan. Though they invoke mixed reactions, they always induce fear in humans. The Roman guards at Jesus' empty tomb flee from the site in deadly terror, having beheld the angel gleaming as lightning (Matt 28:4). Even when they are a welcome presence, they frighten the faithful. After all, they are holy, and we are not.

The Virgin Mary was elated by the visitation of the angel pronouncing the events surrounding the Savior's birth (Luke 1:5–56)—surely her heart was racing with exuberance and joy—but it wasn't pure delight. She was probably also petrified. It's natural for the king's subjects to feel ill at ease in the face of royalty. Yet whenever and to whomever the holy angels appear, one thing is certain: these powerful warriors always come with a mighty word. For the humble and downtrodden, they bring good tidings of good news and great joy—"do not be afraid" (Luke 1:30); "the LORD is with you" (Judg 6:12); "your prayer has been heard" (Luke 1:13).

Even today, these holy messengers are sent to our side, though normally in less fantastic ways. As messengers, their role has changed too. Since the canonization of the Holy Bible, we have the complete revelation of God. The Lord has given us all that he wants us to know about how he creates, redeems, and sanctifies the world. "Jesus Christ is the same yesterday and today and forever" (Heb 13:8). Anyone who adds or takes away from his words (Rev 22:18–19)—even an iota (Matt 5:18)—will fall under God's righteous judgment. This warning holds especially true for his messengers today, pastors, due to their authority over his flock. Any new message or doctrinal revelation from either angel or pastor is, thus, without divine origin. So "even if we or an angel from heaven should preach to you a gospel contrary to the one we preached to you, let him be accursed" (Gal 1:8). Moreover, "Satan disguises himself as an angel of light" (2 Cor 11:14). In short, the church has the Bible as its source of divine knowledge. The messages that it contains suffice for our Christian walk and ministry.

Angels direct us to God alone for knowledge and help. Accordingly, they are careful in appearing among us, lest we end up worshiping them: "Let no one disqualify you, insisting on asceticism and worship of angels, going on in detail about visions" (Col 2:18). Angels do not expect too much of our attention, because it could easily mislead us to ask for their intercessions instead of

Christ's. God decides when and how his instruments are used. And God gets the glory for all of his works. Even the apostle John was tempted in this regard: "Then I fell down at his feet to worship him, but he said to me, 'You must not do that! I am a fellow servant with you and your brothers who hold to the testimony of Jesus. Worship God' " (Rev 19:10). We don't have personal relationships with them—as some believers and members of the occult attempt to have with spirit guides and the like—but they are still active in our world. We can still count on them to help us rely on God's word.

Believing in Angels Matters

Today the existence of angels is considered a childish notion. Instead, we opt for scientific and psychological explanations for the work of both good and bad angels. Angelic appearances are often dismissed as figments of the imagination. Demonic appearances are treated as unsolved mysteries. Yet the Bible presumes their involvement in our world. Scripture is filled with references to angels. Many of Jesus' miracles involve exorcizing demons. And each episode is recorded for our sake, since God continues to act in miraculous ways today.

When it comes to faith, it doesn't take long before the evil one plants seeds of doubt concerning the most important promises of God. "When they hear, Satan immediately comes and takes away the word that is sown in them" (Mark 4:15). When we doubt the truthfulness of these sacred reports we deprive ourselves of the power and wisdom God grants us through them. We become more vulnerable to spiritual attack. Even pastors who believe in the historicity of the biblical narratives find themselves secretly wondering: "Maybe God worked that way in the biblical era, but does he still work in these ways today?" You cannot face the enemy or reach out to your allies unless you first believe that they exist.

Why are we reluctant to believe that God remains alive and active and that he loves us enough to provide humankind with true and trustworthy Scriptures? Our Heavenly Father provides us with an accurate picture of life's unseen realities so that we can be protected. When pastors doubt, so will their people. Like Paul, we urge our parishioners to "be imitators of me, as I am of Christ" (1 Cor 11:1). When the example that we set is lacking, the sheep we lead become more vulnerable to spiritual attack. They are less equipped for spiritual warfare.

The transcendent God chooses to use holy means to save us. The angels are instrumental, and demons detrimental, to our faith journey—on the straight and narrow road toward eternity. The existence of angels reveals a God who isn't cold and aloof. He doesn't watch us from afar. Our Heavenly Father is intimately involved in the daily lives of average people. And even though our eternal destiny counts the most, God also cares about the mundane details of our every day.

God is not just practical. He is also love. Good parents aren't exclusively concerned about the eventual financial security of their kids but also whether or not they are having a good day *today*. Accordingly, the army of angels of heaven are sent as our helpers in both the long and short run.

Angels as Servants

In addition to being messengers, angels are servants—voluntary ones. Until Christ's return, their highest act of serving God is serving us. After all, although adoration is a natural and appropriate response of a creature toward its creator, God doesn't *need* to be told how wonderful he is. God is self-sufficient. But we aren't. We need God. So out of his great mercy, he does everything necessary to bring us into a living relationship with him. He utilizes the ministry of angels to do this. Just like our highest act of servitude and love is caring for our neighbor, the same is true of the angels' service toward us. "Are they not all ministering spirits sent out to serve for the sake of those who are to inherit salvation?" (Heb 1:14). Their goal is to bring us to salvation and keep us from falling away.

Whereas we have mixed feelings about service, the angels enjoy their ministry. The angels believe perfectly that we are the crown of creation and apple of God's eye (Ps 17:8) and yet aren't jealous in the least. As sixteenth-century devotional writer Johann Gerhard so gracefully put it:

> Because our nature is raised in Christ above all angels and archangels (Eph 1:20, 21; Heb 1:4) … the angels do not refuse to serve us men, in honour of the human nature assumed by Christ. As an entire race is brought to honor by a marriage, so the marriage of the Son of God with humanity has

been restored (Matt 22:2). What wonder,
then, that the angels serve us, since the
Son of God, the Lord of the angels, came
to earth that He might serve us?[6]

Unfortunately, we have doubts about our spiritual significance in the wider cosmic battle. We
fluctuate between overestimating our importance
through pride and undervaluing it through self-pity.
Yet still God loves us, and so do the angels. They
gladly participate with God in his salutary work.
"Just so, I tell you, there is joy before the angels of
God over one sinner who repents" (Luke 15:10).
There's an old saying, "The sinner's tears are the
wine and delicacies of the angels." Angels happily
offer God all the glory for their success in helping
people. Angels boast no empire building in their
ministry. They are satisfied with being humble servants—those that aren't satisfied already rebelled
and fell from heaven long ago. As pastors, we need
to guard ourselves from doing the same: making
the ministry about us and forgetting about those
who we have been called to serve. Seeking to imitate the attitudes of angels and not demons isn't
intuitive to the old Adam, who stalks us until we
enter glory.

Avoiding the Mistake of the Demons

Like people, in the beginning the angels made a choice: to abide in relationship with their Maker or sever themselves from his glorious presence and holy community. Instead of resting in the personal fulfillment offered in God alone, they sought to create their own religion. They tried to build their own church. The demons didn't like their assigned roles. Heaven isn't a prison; God wants his creation to love him back freely. He gives his creatures a choice to remain with him. Adam and Eve's choice was made even before they bit the fruit. Both demons and humans sought to be like God, questioning the value of their identity as creatures and instead aspiring to become creators. Some people today want to be free of the devil's stronghold in their lives, but they don't want God to take his place. Yet everyone is a servant to somebody—a servant to none is a slave to the evil one. True freedom comes by being bound to Christ.[7]

When Lucifer rejected true freedom—the freedom that comes with embracing your God-given identity—and instead become Satan and took a third of the angels with him (Rev 12:4), the remaining angels stayed steadfast in their loyalty to God. Because there are no slaves in the kingdom of God, angels serve their Maker freely, never questioning their status or shunning their createdness. They are content with the fruits of their labor. They continue to give themselves fully to the Triune Lord "whose service is perfect freedom," as one historic prayer, the collect for peace, puts it. While the devil enslaves, God sets free indeed (John 8:36), which he does through his church and his pastors with the aid of angels.

Angels Fight for Us

As pastors we want to ensure that we have aligned ourselves with the right kind of angel. Unlike us servants, the angels have no difficulty keeping watch in their ministry and following the orders of their master. We are wise to let them fight for us and let God work through us, trying not to get in the way of either. We do this by letting go of our pride, our ego, our aspirations—in short, ourselves. "Godliness with contentment is great gain" (1 Tim 6:6). When we sinners think that we deserve a more glorious station in life than the one God has given us—that we have outgrown our congregations, mastered our learning curves, and so forth— we are implying that we have greater potential than God realizes. We imply that we know better than him how to run his kingdom. Frankly, we are never as good at ministry as we think. When we repent of our devilish ways and pray, we let the angels, who are better spiritual warriors than us, do the fighting.

One of the most famous Christian pastors and leaders of the ancient church, St. Athanasius, explains that when God sends us angelic helpers, they always arrive in impressive numbers: "For there are many Archangels, many Thrones, and Authorities, and Dominions, thousands of thousands, and myriads of myriads, standing before Him, ministering and ready to be sent."[8] He describes this massive army as God's dispatch units, ready to be deployed to our aid. Like any army, they are organized, orderly, and follow a rigid chain of command. A beautiful painting, "The Assumption of the Virgin" by Francesco Botticini (1475–76) at the National Gallery London, shows three hierarchies and nine orders of angels and archangels, with each cluster exhibiting different characteristics (see facing page).[9] Yet they are one united band in all of their missions, their primary tasks being to serve God by helping us and to glorify, praise, and adore him in worship.

Although invisible, this glorious army of angels is still active in our world, our lives, and your ministries. "Let them aid us and still let them fight. Lord of angelic hosts, battling for right, till, where their anthems they ceaselessly pour, we with the angels may bow and adore."[10]

Angels Fight with Us

If you have ever been involved with an exorcism (and if you haven't, you're lucky!) there is a sense that there are more than just a few entities in the room. Angels are there—lots of them. The demons fear God's company of holy hosts. This explains why some early Christian rites draw upon the angels for help. Yet praying to Jesus Christ and invoking his name will more than suffice to tear down Satan's wicked works. With Jesus at our side and on the tip of our tongues, we will always succeed in battle. For the demons do not fear the exorcist but rather the presence of Christ.

This is why the exorcists' best tools are the audible reading of holy Scripture and prayer. During these uncommoon events, pastors from traditional church bodies may opt to wear stoles and crucifixes, not as lucky charms but as a way of reminding themselves and everyone else—including the invisible bystanders—that they are in the presence of Jesus Christ. They fight from within the mighty fortress of Christ's office and hide behind his person. In spite of the terrifying and evil bully in the room, the pastor is mindful that he is comfortably crouching behind the Creator of heaven and earth. The moment the pastor forgets where he is and in whose company he is, then he is likely to slip up. Jesus alone can subdue, bind, and shackle unclean spirits (Mark 5:1–13). Much of spiritual warfare can be summarized as trying not to get in the way!

Sometimes, we accidentally try to stand by our own authority rather than that of Christ. We trust in our own abilities. We believe that we have the power in ourselves, and operate in our own stead. It's a dangerous fallacy. You can't face the devil as a sinner. You can't battle him alone. You must engage with him from within the stronghold of Christ's body. Pastors often fear the wrong thing. They fear man instead of God (Matt 10:26–28). They measure success by the standards of worldly wisdom rather than the divine. Even after Jesus' successes—like performing miracles and casting out demons—people still asked him to leave them alone (John 6:66; Matt 8:34). Miracles don't cause faith. The glory of God is hidden.

What are we so afraid of when our ministries don't turn out how we wished, even when we, for the most part, have faithfully served? We can do all the right things and still end up with a ministry that, from a human perspective, isn't adequate. When our ministries do seem to flourish, perhaps we ought to be more concerned, since Jesus promises struggles to the faithful: "Indeed, all who desire to live a godly life in Christ Jesus will be persecuted" (2 Tim 3:12).

The devil often attacks those he feels threatened by. But "blessed are you when others revile you and persecute you and utter all kinds of evil against you falsely on my account" (Matt 5:11). Pastors aren't supposed to be aiming to be popular, nor congregations attractive, by worldly standards: "Woe to you, when all people speak well of you, for so their fathers did to the false prophets" (Luke 6:26). But good times or tough, the outcomes are out of our hands. We can make wise choices about how to interpret our experiences. When we take credit for apparent successes or blame ourselves for apparent failures, we have chosen to make the holy and apostolic pastoral ministry about ourselves. We have basically made ourselves into gods. We have succumbed to the same temptation as those fallen angels.

Confronting Demons

Whether you like it or not, part of your call is to practice the ministry of deliverance. Pastors always need to address the demons in people's lives head on. Don't panic when they are uglier than you had anticipated—you have the tools for this kind of specialized ministry. Again, you are already doing it: whenever you baptize people or convert them to the faith, an exorcism of sorts occurs as the Lord delivers those individuals "from the domain of darkness" and transfers them "to the kingdom of his beloved Son" (Col 1:13). Whenever you tell members that Jesus is their Lord and that Christ is victor over their lives, the demons shudder in terror and flee from the hearts they burden (Jas 2:19). But when it comes to demonic possession—which is more common in countries where occult practices are tolerated or pagan religions dominate—pastors feel overwhelmed. Confronting such situations does require a high degree of courage and pastoral sensitivity. Yet because Jesus is the exorcist, the solution and tools always remain the same: prayer and reciting the word of God.

Spiritual oppression—generally the result of people dabbling in the occult but also a consequence of immoral lifestyles, drug abuse, and interest in false teachings and religions—can be difficult to detect. Often, we don't make the connections between parishioner's, say, drug or pornographic addiction, and spiritual influences, since our measures of assessment are largely based on urban myths or Hollywood. These rarely treat demonism as a matter of degrees. One may suffer from demonic oppression and not full-fledged posession. Unless someone manifests physical monstrosities or terrifying voices, we might assume that they're just having a bad day. Certain signs of demonic oppression include the inability to speak the name of our Lord or pray.[11] Even so, unless symptoms are clearly supernatural, most Western Christians remain skeptical. We are inclined to attribute unusual behavior to mental or psychological factors. Some biblical scholars hold that accounts of demonic possession in the New Testament can be ascribed to epilepsy, and thus are purely scientifically explainable. The Bible does not support such claims in the least. Neither do the eyewitness accounts of missionaries today.

Even for pastors who believe that their parishioner may be suffering from demonic ailments, the immediate temptation is to send them away to social workers and secular counselors, who are supposedly better prepared to deal with hurting people. Although medication is a gift of God and many pharmaceuticals can support those recovering from demonic attacks at different levels, there are no remedies that mental health can offer for cases when spiritual illness is manifested in physical forms. In some countries, medical professionals are happy to work with Christian clergy in treating patients who appear to be spiritually oppressed or demonically possessed. In Italy, the Vatican is regularly sought out to help treat those who are hospitalized with symptoms that clearly do not stem from natural causes. In highly secularized countries, pastors don't have this luxury. Even worse, clergy who believe in demoniacs are labeled fanatics. Exorcists are seen as witch doctors.

Even the medical community is mystified by the shocking behavior of some psychiatric patients. I suspect that many experienced practitioners are tempted to attribute the illness at least partially to spiritual causes, while the more myopic ones dismiss what they do not understand to the realm of parapsychology. For both, their lack of faith in religious truth claims prevents them from incorporating nonscientific factors in their diagnoses.

The Christian church shouldn't be shocked by manifestations of the supernatural but rather expect them. Christians have even compiled checklists to assist in their own diagnostics. When two or more of the following symptoms are evident, a red flag should definitely be raised: horrific shouting; bodily contortion or deformation; supernatural events surrounding their person and body; extraordinary abilities and superhuman strength; the knowledge of foreign languages that they have never studied; unusual fits of rage; inability to speak certain Scripture passages or gaze upon religious objects; blasphemy of God; jeering at one's neighbor—especially in unfamiliar voices or including immodest laughing, gnashing of teeth, darkened eyes, removal of clothes, or lacerating oneself (Mark 9:20; Luke 8:26–27); unusual injuries on one's body and those of close acquaintances; and forgetfulness of evil and dangerous things done.[12] For our purposes, this list is sufficient.[13] Admittedly, some of the symptoms resemble diagnosable medical conditions—such as multiple personality disorder, bipolar disorder, and schizophrenia—which is why pastors must carefully navigate through these delicate cases with the help of experienced Christian experts in the field. At the same time, I believe that most mental conditions include a spiritual component.

Medical doctors have clearly defined rules and regulations when treating patients. They have the advantage of operating in accordance with the scientific method. The church does not have that luxury, since spiritual warfare isn't science. One of our greatest obstacles in pastoral practice concerning the severely spiritually oppressed or demonically possessed is knowing how to faithfully navigate through largely unknown, unpredictable terrain when spiritual phenomena effect physical realities. To make matters worse, due to the fear resulting from unfamiliarity with these cases, we end up becoming prejudiced toward people in such spiritual bondage, though the solution requires caring for them in the same way as we would anyone else. Love takes time and commitment. Even referring members to specialists doesn't preclude our constant spiritual care and involvement in their lives. Their sins and struggles, although unusual to most, are not unfamiliar to the heavenly hosts. We ought not be afraid to walk with them through their valley of darkness.

Because of the stigma and skepticism within the church toward the subject, the spiritually oppressed or possessed may shy away from you due to fear of judgment. Those who struggle with issues of abuse or sexuality may do the same until they realize that you are compassionate, trustworthy, and believe them. In the New Testament the demoniacs were brought to Jesus at sundown due to shame over who they were and what they had become (Mark 1:32). Yet "perfect love casts out fear" (1 John 4:18). Jesus seeks them out. He welcomes them. He doesn't send them away. He doesn't recommend a good counselor and leave them alone. He is their pastor, and thus he does what he has been sent to do.

Christian denominations may differ as to how to treat the wide spectrum of demonic activity, but hopefully they all agree that the church provides a unique essential service. Whether it involves prayer, rebuke, historical rites, or reading the Bible, at the end of the day, every tactic involves reminding everybody present—visible or invisible—who is in charge: Jesus. If you compare this Great Physician of the soul with a surgeon, then our Lord comes to cut out the evil by convicting us of our sins and then stitching us up again with his consoling gospel message. Each time he does, each time he performs this precious work—and not just on demoniacs!—we have been once again cleansed from our sins and reestablished to his holy presence. This surgeon operates through you on each and every patient in your flock.

Confronting Sins

As every father prefers to praise his children instead of scolding them, every pastor prefers to comfort rather than rebuke his sheep. For instance, when someone is ashamed of their lifestyle choices and repents of their rebellion, it's refreshing to give them care. You can simply preach to them the lovely, happy gospel: that God accepts them in Jesus Christ and makes them a new creation. Otherwise, before you can deliver the good news, you need to preach judgment in an effort to convince them that God is unhappy with their behavior or attitude. Sin can't be willfully ignored in God's kingdom. John the Baptizer didn't hold back, even though it cost him his life.

There are worse things than death for pastors called to take up their cross and follow the Lord. Lack of courage is one of them. We are not permitted to deprive God's people of the message that he seeks to deliver to them through us. Yet it's a tricky business, discerning when to preach the law versus the gospel; deciding when a reed is actually bruised versus appearing as such, so as not to break it (Isa 42:3). For those two messages, those two tools—the cutting knife of the law, which announces that we have messed up, and the healing stitch of the gospel that God has cleansed it all in Christ—need to be presented in the right order for it to work in accordance with God's design.

The evil angels surely grin with satisfaction when we confuse the two by burdening wounded consciences with an insistence that they exhibit a holier life, or overstating Jesus' mercy to the arrogant and self-righteous who think that they are inherently loveable (Rom 3:12). Just like the prophets of old, pastors are mandated to proclaim both the bad news and the good news, whether people like it or not (2 Tim 4:2). And although pastors are not apostles (the Twelve had a unique role to play in the mission of the church), every pastor is apostolic: whatever we do and say within our office carries apostolic authority. The apostles stand beside us. Jesus is at work within us: "The one who hears you hears me" (Luke 10:16). God trusts us with locking the sins of the unrepentant and unlocking the sins of the repentant with the keys of heaven (John 20:22–23). This operation is a function of the church, given to its leaders for the sake of the congregation. It is powerfully and generously carried on through apostolic ministry via pastors.

Incidentally, this is why, in many churches, the sermons begin and end with Pauline salutations and benedictions. It shows the continuity between the pastoral acts of the past and present. Pastors *sound* like the disciples when they address their congregations from the pulpit with their same words and teachings. After all, the apostles' letters were the church's first sermons! Pastors from liturgical traditions try to dress in a way that not only hides themselves in the clothing of Christ but that also strives to be identical to their other colleagues in the ministry. They hope that their hearers visually comprehend that there aren't a series of different messages of God being professed—only one word for all times and all places (Eph 4:5). The work given to the disciples to "heal the sick, raise the dead, cleanse lepers, cast out demons" (Matt 10:8) carries on today. These miraculous acts aren't always experienced in our bodies. But they are in our souls. We are always spiritually delivered from the illness and uncleanliness of sin through the name of Jesus. The demons tremble in terror when we believe that God's word does exactly what it says. We raise the dead whenever the forgiveness of sins is pronounced.

Believing that pastors aren't making decisions governed by personal opinions but rather by divine inspiration is a huge relief in that difficult case of "handing people over to Satan" from time to time (1 Tim 1:20; 1 Cor 5:5)—that is, practicing church discipline or excommunication. Yet even in those cases when a member is released into the devil's clutches temporarily, the devil isn't in control. In such situations, only a congregation that really believes the pastor has been sent by God will support him when an affluent, active member is placed under discipline. God is doing it for his own good and that of the greater community. It's not an exertion of power but an expression of love.

For this reason, because clergy carry on the apostolic office, having power and authority over the Satanic realm (Luke 9:1; Mark 16:17; Rom 16:20), they do even greater things than exorcizing demons. For forgiving sins and restoring people to a right relationship with God is greater than healing any physical disease. As Jesus says: "Which is easier, to say, 'Your sins are forgiven,' or to say, 'Rise and walk'?" (Matt 9:5). God carries out his ministry of reconciling fleshly physical creatures with him in a fleshly physical world. The kingdom of God continues to live and powerfully move and expand through his called and ordained servants in both direct and indirect ways.

Making the Devil Uncomfortable

Australian theologian John Kleinig summarizes the two principles of effective spiritual warfare against demons to what he calls the "rat principle." If you want to exterminate rats in your house, you do it by both poisoning them directly and then making it uncomfortable for them to stay.[14] The importance of these indirect measures should never be underestimated. Demons hate the rebukes that come with the audible speaking of the word. At the same time, keep them away by surrounding yourself with God's word and rejoicing in it.

A man to whom I provided pastoral care claimed to live in a haunted house. In spite of the house blessings, the ghosts didn't disappear. Consequently, he obsessed over objects that moved around in the day and went thump in the night. In the end I counseled him to ignore the noises and shift his attention to the good things in his life. For example, he had a healthy and lovely family, who, incidentally, weren't as rattled by it all as he was. Without a doubt, the devil was playing an agonizing game with him; it was ultimately harmless, annoying at worst. Yet still it was eroding his home life. I told him that it was his choice as to the outcome. I encouraged him to adopt a more disciplined, and thus richer, family devotion time. I prodded him to invite into his home more deliberately Christian sights and sounds—hymn singing during his daily devotions, as well as speaking to Jesus aloud and in the words of Scripture throughout the day. I instructed him to decorate his home in a way that visually reinforced his faith, such as by hanging up pictures of Jesus, crosses, and crucifixes. After all, the cross is a terror to hell. As one nineteenth-century pastor, C. F. W. Walther, put it:

It shines upon its ruins as a sign of the victory over sin, death, and Satan. With a crushed head, the serpent of temptation lies at the foot of the cross. It is a picture of eternal comfort on which the dimming eye of the dying longingly looks, the last anchor of his hope and the only light that shines in the darkness of death.[15]

Images of the cross not only strengthen despairing Christians but also help to scare away their demons. My advice to include some visual reminders of Jesus in the home was not driven by superstition. It stirred up more Christian conversation and prayer in the household, to the frustration, undoubtedly, of those vexing demonic entities. We all need to be constantly reminded of who owns our lives, homes, and families. The moment we stop hearing that God is in charge, we inadvertently open a door to the devil. The evil one isn't interested in residing in such uncomfortable spaces for long, especially when he senses that everybody knows that he is defeated (Rev 12:8). We conquer him with faith; "no, in all these things we are more than conquerors through him who loved us" (Rom 8:37).

CHAPTER 4

Angelic Warriors
and Pastors

*In many and various ways, God spoke to His people
of old by the prophets, but now in these last days,
He has spoken to us by His Son.*
—Hebrews 1:1–2, Responsory for Evening Prayer

THE NEW TESTAMENT ENCOURAGES CONGRE-
gations to receive their pastors as angels of God (Gal
4:14). Most exegetes have concluded that "angels
of the seven churches," to whom the message of
Revelation is addressed, is a reference to the bishops
and leaders of those seven churches (Rev 1:20). This
exhilarating comparison should not go to our heads:
"Nevertheless, do not rejoice in this, that the spirits
are subject to you, but rejoice that your names are
written in heaven" (Luke 10:20).

We shouldn't be surprised that we are compared to angels according to our divine office. We do a similar work. Just as angels are sent to do the Lord's work and speak the Lord's word, so are pastors. We are there to defend, protect, and help our people. The voices of pastors preaching and teaching thunder like the angels in the spiritual kingdoms in which they serve. "The voice of the LORD is powerful; the voice of the LORD is full of majesty" (Ps 29:4). Both angels and pastors are unique mouthpieces and instruments of God.

PASTORS ARE ANGELS TO
THEIR CONGREGATIONS

To help convince and encourage you in the notion that you are like the angels, I have a devised a little exercise. In the following words of St. Chrysostom, I invite you to replace the word "angel" and references to them as servants with "pastor," and you will view yourself in a new light:

Are they not all ministering spirits, sent forth to minister for them who shall be heirs of salvation?" What marvel (saith he) if they minister to the Son, when they minister even to our salvation? See how He lifts up their minds, and shows the great honor which

God has for us, since He has assigned to Angels who are above us this ministration on our behalf. As if one should say, for this purpose (saith he) He employs them; this is the office of Angels, to minister to God for our salvation. So that it is an angelical work, to do all for the salvation of the brethren: or rather it is the work of Christ Himself, for He indeed saves as Lord, but they as servants. And we, though servants are yet Angels' fellow-servants. Why gaze ye so earnestly on the Angels (saith he)? They are servants of the Son of God, and are sent many ways for our sakes, and minister to our salvation.[16]

Angels minister to us, and we minister as angels to others. What a beautiful pattern. From love flows love. Just like God equips angels, so he equips us. Angels, pastors, and all Christians have the tools to fight the good fight (1 Tim 6:12). And the most effective tactical strategy is pretty straightforward: telling everybody the truth.

EXORCISING WITH THE TRUTH

Contrary to common depictions by popular culture and the movies, exorcisms are not supposed to look like theatrical magic shows, with shouts and incantations. Exorcists are not Christianized witch doctors. A real exorcism of the demonically possessed—which is not, by any stretch of the imagination, explainable simply with psychology—is characterized by truth telling. The exorcizing pastor tells everyone—especially the devil—the timeless, essential truth: the evil one doesn't belong. The pastor also tells the victim the truth: that God loves them. They belong to God as his adopted children through Jesus Christ (Eph 1:5). Much of the ministry of deliverance is delivering all the participants such biblical messages.

When dealing with those oppressed or possessed by demons, never understate the power of reminding everyone of their true identity: that they belong to God. The demons can't have them. The devil is a mere creature under the authority of Christ. He doesn't call the shots. He is a liar and a thief. He is powerless before Christ. He attempts to possess that which is not his. Because nothing actually belongs to any creature, the devil cannot possess anything. Instead, he steals, and he pretends that he owns something. But Satan is not the Lord of any space or place, even hell itself. Rather he is its greatest subject and slave. Thus, this masterful deceiver remains metaphysically dissatisfied, restless and unfulfilled outside of the life of his Creator. He greedily and desperately looks inward for fulfillment, yearning to create and own—to possess. Even though he wants to possess houses, objects, and people, in actuality he can only occupy them for a moment. Ultimately, he is a mere impotent thief, because he can create nothing; he can possess nothing.

That is why our baptismal identity—the fact that we are children of God—is crucial to counseling those who are physically oppressed or possessed by demons. This objective brings us back to the fact that we have been purchased and won "from all sins, from death, and from the power of the devil; not with gold or silver, but with his holy, precious blood and with his innocent suffering and death, that [we] may be his own and live under him in his kingdom," as Martin Luther put it so well.[17] The Holy Spirit has made our hearts Christ's home through his holy word and gracious ways. The devil needs to be told and reminded that the Holy Spirit is the owner. Although this is true of all people, since Christ died for everyone, it is especially so in the case of Christians, who are the temples of the Holy Spirit. So, the pastor rebukes these trespassers with

God's efficacious word: "Be gone, Satan" (Matt 4:10), or "depart unclean spirit and make room for the Holy Spirit."[18]

Similarly, ghosts are squatters in God's buildings. House blessings and rebukes during exorcisms remind these robbers of this crucial fact, which is why they are forced to flee. The Chief Shepherd's words to Peter—"Get behind me, Satan! You are a hindrance to me. For you are not setting your mind on the things of God, but on the things of man" (Matt 16:23)—are not just for his own use but intended to be used by the church at large. When pastors speak them, it is Christ who is heard. "But when the archangel Michael, contending with the devil, was disputing about the body of Moses, he did not presume to pronounce a blasphemous judgment, but said, 'The Lord rebuke you' " (Jude 1:9). Rebuking the devil is for all those who practice the angelic ministry: both angels and pastors!

Pastors may be tempted to encourage downhearted Christians by trying to build up their self-esteem. But this can be a treacherous refuge in their struggles. Instead, returning to our identity in Christ is the only way we can fully appreciate the meaning and value of a life. After all, we are esteemed by God for the sake of our loving Savior, who counts us of great and precious worth. The lying devil wants us to believe that this is not true—that our worth and purpose is subjective. Pastoral care and counseling of all kinds is about helping people remember who they are in Christ. A deepened faith and commitment to their vocational responsibilities and obligations will naturally follow.

Many Christians also find tracing the sign of the cross from head to heart and shoulder to shoulder, to be a helpful tool in trying circumstances; it reminds us that we belong to Jesus. The majority of spiritual victories can be reduced to believing this simple phrase: "I belong to Jesus." It's a fact that the demons cannot dispute. When spoken in faith from a believing heart, it's a word from which they always flee.

Discerning the Spirits of False Teaching

Lies are the devil's main strategy to subdue us. He lies about who God is, how he has saved us, and who we are in Christ. Casting doubt on our identity in Christ is his most effective way of discouraging us, because it tortures our conscience and can even lead us to despair. We could thus surmise that Satan's key weapon is false teaching. False teaching covers all this territory. Repeatedly, this architect of false religion and highly skilled manipulator twists, perverts, and poisons the truth with the goal of getting us to doubt who God says we are in Christ. Spiritual warfare always involves discerning spirits. That means weighing the truth of faith claims, doctrinal content, scriptural interpretation, and so forth. All these things influence our understanding of our Christian identity; "beloved, do not believe every spirit, but test the spirits to see whether they are from God, for many false prophets have gone out into the world" (1 John 4:1).

The devil's most dangerous deceptions attack our beliefs about who we are. Consider our sexual or gender identity and our identity as redeemed sinners. Regarding our status as men and women, God made male and female as two different but beautiful ways of existing as human beings in caring for the earth. Yet the devil misleads us telling us that our sex is just another physical attribute among many others. Falsely believing that your sex is not pertinent to your human identity—like the shape of your nose or the color of your eyes—and that you can choose your gender results in living a lie and a denial of your God-given identity. Regarding our status as sinners, the evil one convinces us that we are morally superior to others and don't need church—the holy means through which our Creator communes with us. The devil whispers that we can be our own pastors, our own shepherds, our own messiahs—our own gods. Regarding our status as saints: Satan, "your adversary" (1 Pet 5:8) and "accuser" (Rev 12:10), is masterfully crafty at accusing us of our sins. He lies about the value that we have in Christ (Matt 10:29–30), enticing us to dwell on our sins as if they were unforgiven and insisting that God's unconditional love for us is a fraud. Ultimately the devil's lies about our identity lead to spiritual confusion and psychological misery.

Battling Demons with the Word of Truth

Much of the literature on exorcism talks about the importance of determining demons' so-called entry points. The devil looks for opportunities to enter into our hearts, minds, and souls through these various struggles and emotions. The enemy clouds our reasoning abilities and tempts us to look for quick fixes to our problems, convincing some that their only resort is drugs, alcohol, or other vices. Knowing the demons' source can help target them and cast them away.

However, in my experience, it doesn't need to be that complicated. While knowing the entry point can help a pastor lead the afflicted person through repentance, ultimately God knows how the demons entered and how to get rid of them. The best exorcism rituals or ceremonies are simply reciting Scripture and biblical prayers. The exorcist basically silences our spiritual enemies with the truth.

As a military chaplain, I often listened to suicidal soldiers who were struggling with mental and spiritual illnesses tell me that they did not want to die, but they just wanted to make the pain stop—the tormenting memories, hounding nightmares, endless guilt, and unbearable shame—but didn't know how. The devil likes to take our feelings of guilt and shame and spin them bigger and bigger. The devil is a murderer and a liar, and this is his goal: to drag us to hell with him. He does this primarily by leading people to believe that they are not precious, redeemed creatures of our loving and forgiving Lord Jesus Christ. In the end, the ultimate purpose of demonic lies is not to possess you for a moment, harass you for a while, nor depress you for a season, but to demolish you, God's beloved creatures, in body and soul. Demons want you to join them in their eternal misery both now and forever. Thus, the devil is a "murderer" (John 8:44) who holds people "in slavery by their fear of death" (Heb 2:14–15 NIV). At the end of the day, the demons seek death for all. They want us to experience death in our lives, in our identities, in our vocations, and in all of our relationships with God and others.

Demonic Manifestations: Obvious and Subtle

In cases of suicide, pastoral intervention pivots upon addressing and correcting false identities. People who want to kill themselves lack faith in who God says they are, that God has redeemed them and loves them, and that their worth is found in him.

In some ways, staring into the eyes of a victim of demonic oppression is easier than confronting the devil in his more subtle manifestations—in his lies and partial truths—because there aren't a lot of responses besides prayers and rebukes on which to rely. The words do not take much imagination; you just recite Scripture. An exorcism is usually over in a few minutes or hours. It's easier than providing long-term counseling, care, and relationship to struggling, oppressed, and suffering parishioners. Sometimes this counseling can go on for years. Long-term pastoral commitment to troubled parishioners requires patience and problem-solving stamina. The aftercare that pastors provide to a demoniac is more intense and involved than the events of the actual exorcism. But even there, at least the devil's ways are somewhat predictable and the pastoral solution is clear. Most of our encounters with the devil are in the seemingly mundane problems in our lives and those of our members. Fighting Satan here is trickier. Providing counsel and offering advice takes some creative thinking and lots of prayer.

The devil's daily tactics are subtle, and Christians may need some convincing that they are dangerously real. In our irrational age, in which absurd subjective truths are no longer debated but simply taken for granted, the gods of scientism rule with unquestioned authority. The veracity of biblical claims are treated with increasing suspicion in pluralistic societies that pride themselves on their supposed open-mindedness.

Pastors today find themselves not only surrounded by a shocking degree of biblical illiteracy but also by an utter deficiency in critical thinking. People increasingly try to discern truth with their feelings and intuitions. Many pastors are compelled to devote some of their Bible study time to teaching people how to think logically as a necessary prerequisite to mature Bible study and full appreciation of the theological nuances of sermons.

The laity are entrenched in a culture that is antagonistic toward the objective truths of Christianity. Emotions and feelings override rational discourse in the public sphere. Our people are torn by mixed allegiances. Pastors feel the added pressure of being educators and convincing people of basic Christian truths. When they encounter irrationality in public debate, government policy, and church meetings, pastors detect newly devised, devilish influences upon well-meaning people. Reason is a gift of God to the world. When it is disregarded or used improperly, it can be as destructive as any other devilish weapon.

PASTORS PARTNER AS
ANGELIC MESSENGERS

Because we are Christ's ambassadors, the angels are sent to help us. They are preoccupied with all that we do as we minister together in the kingdom of God. The difference is that they are holy, and we are sinners. So they never get discouraged, whereas we do all the time, because we are our own worst enemies. If we fully trusted God, we wouldn't beat ourselves up when the congregational meeting didn't unfold as we had hoped and prayed. We would trust that we have given our people the tools to fight on their own, even when they resist our instruction or dismiss it as one option among many others.

We may only get a couple of hours each week to override the satanic voices of the world with Christ's voice in worship and Bible study. Yet never underestimate the importance of those holy conversations. Just as the walls of Jericho shattered with a shout and a trumpet blas, the walls behind which our enemies cower will tumble each time a pastor proclaimes the gospel . "With God we shall do valiantly; it is he who will tread down our foes" (Ps 60:12). Every faithful pastor is a mighty messenger of God's truths, even when he feels that his Spirit-filled words fall upon deaf ears. Like angels, pastors are helpers to those entrusted to their care, even when unappreciated.

Most pastors do not see themselves as kings ruling over their people. Rather, they consider themselves simply as servants, as shepherds watching over their flock at night, as disciples called to wash the feet of their people by proclaiming the forgiveness of sins and God's unconditional love to them. The shepherd's relentless dedication to his flock often goes unacknowledged by his sheep. Yet that doesn't stop most of them from esteeming the beautiful proclamation and mindboggling teaching that their incarnate Lord continues to draw near them through their pastors.

Many pastors are increasingly taking the time to teach about pastoral ministry. Reestablishing the value of ministry in the eyes of parishioners allows them to better perceive the miraculous and gracious work of God at work *for them* through their pastors. Too many pastors allow themselves to be perceived as hired hands, and when they are, they can easily be taken advantage of and evaluated according to the wrong—that is, worldly—criteria.

Pastoral authority goes hand in hand with servanthood. God exemplified this when he gave his only Son, the Chief Shepherd and highest of priests, for the life of the world and for every one of his precious children. The King of kings became the servant of all. When Jesus says, "Whoever would be great among you must be your servant" (Matt 20:26), he is not only admonishing his pastors but describing them!

Jesus asks us to imitate him. He sends his Spirit to enable us to prioritize others, as he has so graciously prioritized us. He calls us to act like angels.

It's a thankless job being a pastor, putting others first, especially when nobody notices except God and his holy angels. But it remains our calling nevertheless— our vocation, identity, and destiny. Angels don't mind the role that they play. Why do we?

The wicked angels want us to mind. They tempt us to view ourselves as prisoners to a domineering master instead of imitators of the Good Shepherd. Our parishioners are often tempted to think of their pastors in a similar manner. Children often think of their earthly fathers that way too: "Why is my private life his business? It's my life and my choice." And so, the evil angels distract us from what others would consider mundane, thankless service and tempt us to make more of it, which means making more of ourselves. The devil speaks through human voices tempting us to doubt who we are as pastors. They say things like, "Pastor, you share the same gospel week after week. Can't you talk about something else? What about giving us more practical tips on how to live better lives?" Instead we pray that God would forgive them and us for these immature patterns of thinking, which assume that successful ministry involves more than simply spreading the message of Jesus. The work is difficult because we want to make more of it than God does. It is his ministry, not ours. When we believe that, being faithful to his word becomes the main criteria for being a good pastor.

Even though God doesn't have to, he chooses to partner with us. Perhaps one reason he does so is to keep us humble, seeing that nothing is dependent upon our works when it comes to the heavenly kingdom, "to show that the surpassing power belongs to God and not to us" (2 Cor 4:7). This partnership also keeps us together as a community, preventing us from seeing ourselves as independent. In the unequal distribution of gifts and abilities, he forces us to rely on each other, to practice the forgiveness of sins. He also prepares his people on earth for the community of heaven. He prepares all Christians to live with angels and in angelic ways. In Christian community at its best, we get a taste of what is to come in the heavenly Jerusalem. We are being made ready for our new home.

In contrast to heaven, hell is filled with individualists, lonely people stuck living together. Hell is for the devil, but its doors are open to those who want to join him. If hell is, as Satan likes to advertise it, ultimate freedom, it is freedom from the beauty of creation, freedom from divine goodness, and freedom from true, eternal community between

God and others. It is also freedom from all that our bodies enjoy: light, taste, smells. Hell isn't a big party. It is a desolate place. It is a great misconception that the demons rule hell. They are its greatest prisoners. "God did not spare angels when they sinned, but cast them into hell and committed them to chains of gloomy darkness to be kept until the judgment" (2 Pet 2:4). Yet typical to his character, the devil disseminates partial truths with evil intent. Such lies are more effective, since they echo the thoughts of our own old Adam. The demons know what we all want to hear. But the angels know what we all *need* to hear.

THE ANGEL OF THE LORD WITH YOU

The Scriptures tell of one special angel that is unlike any others: the angel of the Lord. We encounter him during the captivity of the three men of God in the fiery furnace; the angel envelops them with his merciful protection (Dan 3:25). We find him and his mighty sword with David at Gibeon (1 Chr 21:30). He is not only the mouthpiece of God but functions as God in the calling, testing, and blessing of Abraham (Gen 22:1–19). Most Christians have considered this to be a name for the Second Person of the Trinity, who appeared in biblical history numerous times before his incarnation as Jesus. When you look at his actions and words, it's a convincing argument. It's also encouraging—you are not only surrounded and supported by God's angels but also the Son of God.

For Christians in general and pastors in particular, this angel abides in you and continues to carry out his angelic services through you! Appreciating how (or the fact that) the angel of the Lord is at work through our pastors would change the way we treat them when we disagree on matters of clear doctrine. It would also change the way pastors treat their colleagues when they have differences of opinion. As St. Paul writes: "Though my condition was a trial to you, you did not scorn or despise me, but received me as an angel of God, as Christ Jesus" (Gal 4:14). What immense comfort comes from recognizing that Christ, the Angel of angels, shares his power, wisdom, and might with his faithful followers. Some Protestants are rattled by the idea that the rite of ordination may not simply be a symbolic communal authorization of a clergyman to operate on the congregation's behalf, but that it may offer him some special quality. Yet if ordination does impart special spiritual graces, it isn't for the pastor's own sake. It is always for the sake of those to whom he has been called to serve—for the sake of the larger church. Being called and ordained means being set aside for use by the Son of God.

Lest we become puffed up with this sacred authority, a humorous account in Numbers 22 can act as a humbling description of the holy office of the ministry. The angel of the Lord appears to Balaam, yet he uses a donkey to preach (Num 22:28). Whenever I teach at our mission sites in Latin America—where donkeys are viewed as dumb, common, and clumsy animals—the students get a chuckle from comparing God's pastors with such creatures. The holy office isn't about the intelligence or eloquence of the one holding the office. When Jesus rides triumphantly into Jerusalem on that first Palm Sunday (Matt 21:1–11), the focus is on the rider and not the vehicle. It's still that way today. Jesus chooses his instrument according to his divine wisdom and grace. "Oh, the depth of the riches and wisdom and knowledge of God! How unsearchable are his judgments and how inscrutable his ways!" (Rom 11:33). We are called by grace. Being a pastor isn't a question of who can do the job best. God selects. And he often carries on an ancient custom of using the foolish and weak in this world to shame the wise and strong (1 Cor 1:27). He uses humble instruments to nourish his people. As he tells Peter, "Feed my sheep" (John 21:17). God not only shares his authority but also his power with us. When the masses ran out of food, he tells his disciples, "*You* give them something to eat" (Mark 6:37, emphasis mine). In the Old Testament, God sent his people manna, and "man ate of the bread of the angels" (Ps 78:25). If Jesus is that manna—"the bread of God is he who comes down from heaven and gives life to the world" (John 6:33)—then pastors are at their best when they simply offer God's people "the bread of life" (John 6:35) through faithful preaching, teaching, and ministry.

The Angel of the Lord in You

The angel of the Lord lives in you and through your office. We find him in your fiery furnaces, gripping the same sword that has been placed in your hand. He is the same one through whose crucifixion, suffering, and death came the total destruction of the devil's works and plans.

When we allow these deep truths to take root in our pastoral hearts, the joy of pastoral service returns, in spite of the biting words and aggravating perspectives of our adversaries. We remember that we are like the angels in our spiritual warfare. We recall that we stand with the angels in every one of our battles. For Christian joy is deeper than happiness. Truth surpasses feeling. Even criticisms then become opportunities to speak the blessed truth, though we still suffer and lose sleep because of them.

Remember that the shape of the pastoral office, and our reactions within the battles set before us, are determined by how much we allign our servanthood with that of the angels—the degree to which we want to be characterized as messengers of good news, offering sabbath rest, loosening our sheep from enchainment to false teachings or worldviews. Like the angel who set Peter free from his prison (Acts 12:5–11), we release our people from bondage. And even when they are not fully convinced by our words, we do not agonize over perceived failures, keeping a record of their sins. God doesn't keep such a tally, so neither do we. Instead, we choose to remember the message that we seek to convey to others, and we preach it to ourselves. It always bears a harvest of fruit in both shepherd and sheep.

This is the joy that comes only through forgiveness of sins—ours and theirs. For Christ, the angel of the Lord, dwells within you.

CHAPTER 5

The Word and Armor of God

For this holy house and for all who offer here
their worship and praise, let us pray to the Lord.
Lord, have mercy.
—From the Litany in Evening Prayer

It is no accident that God likens Christian ministry to physical combat. He calls Christians "soldiers" (2 Tim 2:3). It's a key biblical analogy for explaining the struggles that pastors undergo in their public ministry and that all Christians deal with in their lives. In the kingdom of God, there are two kinds of soldiers: angels and Christians. Both operate under the command of our Triune God. Though possessing different skill sets and roles, angels and Christians fight together in coordinated efforts against our common enemy, the devil. Yet angels have an advantage over us: they get to see the battle from a bird's-eye view. For them, it is crystal clear who is the victor. We are stuck assessing the situation from a worm's-eye vantage point, crawling around in the wet and muddy trenches of our daily trials. Our vision is limited by our personal experiences and subjective perceptions. It's not as clear to us that God is in control. God knows that, and so he offers us help: spiritual gear.

The gear that we need to engage in spiritual warfare—the armor and weapons described by St. Paul in Ephesians 6:10–18—is so important to the cosmic battle that God ensures that we are equipped with it all. Whether it be the belt of truth, the breastplate of righteousness, the shield of faith, the helmet of salvation, or the sword of the Spirit, Christians take and receive what has already been achieved for them by Jesus Christ at his victorious cross. Jesus gives us the same top-of-the-line heavenly equipment that he used and perfected while he battled for us on earth, defeating the evil one once and for all.

The Bible says, "Put on the whole armor of God, that you may be able to stand against the

schemes of the devil" (Eph 6:11), as though don-
ning the appropriate military attire were up to us.
But in a mysterious way, it is God who dresses us
and equips us for battle. Our role is to "give no
opportunity to the devil" (Eph 4:27)—treasuring
our armor by learning how to use it.

Although God's equipment works perfectly
well, we still need training. Lifelong training begins
through preaching, Bible study, and catechesis.
Leaders go to seminary. Pastors arm themselves
with the word of God when they diligently study
theology, and then train others by sharing all that
they have received through the holy church. This
is how they prepare the flock for service, "to equip
the saints for the work of ministry, for building up
the body of Christ, until we all attain to the unity
of the faith and of the knowledge of the Son of God"
(Eph 4:12). Every Christian is crucial in the battles
that we face together. Pastors are unique in the operations. They not only fight; they also train. They
lead and equip the laity for warfare (Eph 4:12–16).

The two most important lessons learned in
this field are: First, that God's gear is given to us
by grace. Second, that it is primarily for *defensive*
rather than *offensive* use. One way that pastors feed
their sheep (John 21:17) is by helping each of their

lambs believe that they are under the complete protection of the Chief Shepherd of their souls, Jesus Christ, despite the wolves by which they know they are surrounded.

God's Gear Is Given

The careful language that St. Paul uses in describing Christian soldiering as being clothed in the full armor of God reinforces that the holy ministry isn't about us or something that we do. Not only does God's equipment work well (even when we don't!), it is a gift.

Some Christians feel like they need to beg the Holy Spirit to give them what they lack or spend hours of intense prayer pleading with God to spare clues in their quest for spiritual gifts. This makes our salvation more about us and what we think we must do to spiritually survive, rather than what Christ has done for us. The reception of our equipment is best compared with the shower of gifts bestowed on children at Christmas morning from kind and generous parents. Every Christian receives his or her complete kit through their baptism.

Similarly, some pastors believe that if they just prayed a little harder, or begged a little more, God would give them more of the talents that they need to make their churches better. When caring for souls, pastors are often tempted to interpret the perceived successes or failures of their ministry as reflections of how well they personally are equipped for their vocation. The struggle centers on the question: To whom does the ministry belong? But it isn't ours. It belongs to Christ. Burnout and compassion fatigue are often the results of taking ministry too personally. When the forecasted results of faithful ministry seem to be lacking, we either develop a martyr complex, or we blame ourselves. We try harder, and harder, and harder. Sometimes we despair and give up. We blame God.

Truth be told, when we feel ill-equipped to serve, we are actually better off than when we feel confident in our ministry. How? We are less tempted to rely upon our own perceived gifts, abilities, and skills in the battle. After all, as the crucifixion clearly demonstrates, our eyes and experiences can deceive us. God's power is hidden in what looks like defeat; his "power is made perfect in weakness" (2 Cor 12:9).

Sometimes God tears down a ministry or even closes a church (!) as part of his strategic plan. Whether we agree with these events or not, whether we understand them or not, God makes the best decisions. As Dietrich Bonhoeffer wrote: "We do not know his plan. We cannot see whether he is building or pulling down. It may be that the times which by human standards are times of collapse are for him the great times of construction. It may be that the times which from a human point of view are great times for the church are times when it is pulled down."[19]

When our church doesn't grow, it's not necessarily our fault. Neither do we get the credit when it does flourish. In short, *our* people are actually *God's* people. The challenges of ministry are ultimately his problems, not ours. That doesn't mean that we don't take ownership and responsibility for our mistakes—but we do not beat ourselves up over our failures or the unexpected and unwelcome results of faithful ministry.

When we faithfully serve by simply doing the work that we have been asked to do, we become less irritated when our members suffer physically or deteriorate spiritually in spite of all of our faithful visits to them and diligent prayers for them. "Neither he who plants nor he who waters is anything, but only God who gives the growth" (1 Cor 3:7). That means that we can step away from our parishes during those moments when the burden seems too heavy. God didn't make a mistake when he matched you with your congregation. We don't need to overthink our decisions or agonize over our errors when we trust that our merciful and almighty God is in control. Only God knows how the stories unfold for those who have let us down or vice versa. Instead, we repent, pray, and believe in God's goodness, grace, and forgiveness.

Imagine if the angels treated their ministry to us as if they owned it themselves! Imagine the self-induced frustration they would undergo in guarding and defending us in our constantly foolish decision-making. Instead, they don't worry. They are not disheartened. They simply worship God joyfully and keep soldiering along. Why? Because they trust God.

Whenever a church perpetuates a cult of personality around the pastor—where the congregation's or ministry's stability, strength, or well-being is attributed to the charisma, skills, and gifts of the pastor—the pastor lives in a kind of existential self-contradiction, to his and his congregation's detriment. Even though pastors are stewards of their master's goods (Titus 1:7), they behave as if they run the place.

Some church traditions have unique furniture—like pulpits, lecterns, and altars—to remind us that even though we are at home at church, we are not in our own house. Every altar is also a supper table from which God feeds his people. The pastor serves, but he's not the chef! The liturgical dress that some pastors wear—such as albs, cassocks, and chasubles—are intended to hide or disguise the individual in the clothing of Christ. Even the clerical collar still worn by many symbolizes that the pastor isn't operating in his own stead but remains an ambassador for Christ (2 Cor 5:20). He is simply our Lord's messenger. Despite everything else—the good, the bad, and the ugly in parish ministry—his mission is to deliver God's word accurately to God's people.

These visual reminders help prevent pastors from growing full of themselves when their churches are popular and successful. More importantly, they help keep pastors from despairing and becoming depressed when their churches are severely attacked within and without or when their ministry seems to be doing poorly and they are blamed.

The constant concern that you haven't done enough to improve the life of the church can easily result in shame over your calling and even lead to serious mental health issues. If I believe that my congregation is a permanent fixture in God's kingdom, or that it needs *me* to advance its ministry, I have made my church and even myself into gods (in other words, something with which we cannot live without).

We all lack faith, and that is why we get so down on ourselves when God's will contradicts our own. In short, we suffer unnecessarily when we seek meaning or a logical explanation to the unwelcome experiences of life in any place other than where God promises to offer it. He tells us what we need to know exclusively in his word.

Take the prophet Gideon for example. What is remarkable about this man of God is how easily he obeyed Yahweh's order, even though he was afraid (Judg 7:10–11) and even when the Lord's word seemed rather crazy: lapping of water, downsizing the army, a dream about barley bread. The outcome was even more mind-boggling: the enemy destroyed itself while Gideon's tiny army stood by watching, armed with nothing but torches, jars, and trumpets (Judg 7:16–18). This one pastor saved his whole congregation by simply trusting God's word.

We are like Gideon when, in spite of our nerves and even the world's common sense, we believe God's word and obey it. These works from faith demolish the dark armies within the spiritual world. Things may continue to appear as if nothing has changed. If only we believed that Gideon's war experience was a paradigmatic example for our pastoral ministry, "for we are his workmanship, created in Christ Jesus for good works, which God prepared beforehand, that we should walk in them" (Eph 2:10). What pastors do, what they say, what they believe have eternal consequences for our people.

When I was a military chaplain, I helped many a broken soldier recovering from PTSD. Pastoral care for them involved reaffirming their faith in their identity as a soldier as meaningful and necessary in spite of the dirty work that it entailed. Once, I provided pastoral care for a soldier who suffered feelings of guilt for killing in battle. Instead of understanding himself as a tool of the state, he took his job too personally. The only way to harmonize conflicting feelings stemming from his identity as a soldier and also as a Christian was learning to see himself in accordance with his vocation. He needed to hide himself within his uniform. Soldiers don't function in their own stead.

That's what pastors need to do, too. Through their office, they hide inside the clothing of Jesus and they teach their members how to hide within the baptismal garment of Christ's robe of righteousness. "So then let us cast off the works of darkness and put on the armor of light. ... But put on the Lord Jesus Christ" (Rom 13:12, 14). We all hide behind Christ, our victor, who not only defends us from the devilish bullies of guilt and discouragement but also reminds us of our identity and mission: who we are, why we fight, and by what authority we operate. We function within the office of pastor. When we forget in whose stead we stand, we suffer unnecessarily from conflicts of interest among our various identities. Even after twenty-one years of ministry, I still find it hard not to take it personally when my pastoral advice is rejected or a parishioner with whom I have become friends abandons the church. I confuse the message with the messenger.

A mature sense of your pastoral identity and function in the kingdom of God is critical to your overall health and peace. When pastors accurately view their vocation as God's calling for them, they not only behave more professionally and with a clearer mind, but they also protect their loved ones from workplace stress. In those hard moments, when the pastor has done all things as faithfully as he is able and in accordance with Scripture's directives, and it has still resulted in a mess, he shifts the responsibility onto Jesus, knowing that he was only doing what he was called to do (Matt 25:21). He serves in another's stead.

When our people witness that their pastors aren't perfect, it also helps direct them to the only one who is: Jesus. Starting with us pastors, Jesus puts our perfectionist tendencies or misplaced work ethic in eternal perspective. In Christ, we interpret all our successes and failures within our vocations from the standpoint of his cross. Our strengths are gifts. Our weaknesses are forgiven. Our sins are covered by the blood of the Lamb. When the spiritual battle goes well, it's the Holy Spirit at work. When it doesn't, it's the same Spirit at work "to forgive us our sins and to cleanse us from all unrighteousness" (1 John 1:9). When we believe that "for those who love God all things work together for good, for those who are called according to his purpose" (Rom 8:28), there is no failure in spiritual war.

God's Gear Is Primarily Defensive

Notice, in St. Paul's description of the full armor of God, how little he asks us to *do* anything. Instead, Christians are to *respond* to attacks from the enemy but not to *move*. He depicts spiritual soldiering in terms of defensive maneuvering. We take what God has given us and stay put wherever we are.

The word "stand"—as in "stand guard"—is used a number of times in the text. The kind of soldier with which St. Paul was familiar while writing from his prison cell was a Roman sentry. These guards stayed in one place and would be executed for treason if they left their post. So too for us: our mighty Lord himself, in accordance with his divine providence, has placed us precisely where he wants us. We are not to move away from our designated post until he says so.

The ordination and installation of pastors into their congregations and ministries is not a result of human processes. Search committees and job interviews are no match for the Holy Spirit. A pastor can take great comfort in the fact that wherever he serves, God has put him there. Thus, until God moves him elsewhere, he is supposed to stand. Guard. Wait. When trouble comes, fight.

Although most of the armor of God is for defensive use, at least one piece is for offense: "the sword of the Spirit, which is the word of God" (Eph 6:17). When conflicts arise and the devil attacks, pastors aren't expected to be passive observers at their post, standing idle like statues. To the contrary, in caring for souls, they are to apply law and gospel rightly to each one of the beloved sheep entrusted to their care. "Preach the word; be ready in season and out of season; reprove, rebuke, and exhort, with complete patience and teaching" (2 Tim 4:2). While pastors choose their battles carefully, some hills are worth dying on, as Jesus exemplified at Golgotha. God knows which ones. The Lord's servants don't seek them, nor do they flee from them. Through prayer "at all times" (Eph 6:18), the Holy Spirit directs them and their deeds.

The shield of faith—a reference to the scutum, a tall Roman shield that rests upon the ground—helps stabilize us,[20] keeping us from swaying in carrying out our pastoral duties. Apathy or indolence is the natural consequence of a lack of faith in who we are and in our mission. Instead, pastors are asked to stand firm, not chasing congregational calls or attractive contracts from churches purely for more job stability, lucrative benefits, or mission opportunities. All of us who have served in the ministry for more than a few years have heard the little voice of the old Adam whisper inside our hearts: "You have outgrown that church. This ministry has become stagnant. God's got something better for you in store."

There isn't much worldly pleasure in staying at our posts, remaining steadfast in the office to which we have been called and placed. Sometimes the church can appear deserted, considering the rate of clergy resignations and career changes that we increasingly witness. The days when kings invited the priests to join them in the royal court are over. Government officials once welcomed our words and prayers. No more. Friendly smiles cast and reverent nodding heads while the local clergy passed by on the street have been replaced by puzzled facial expression from unchurched children or awkward glances from suspicious parents in the malls. Even in churches, the local pastor is no longer overwhelmed by requests for home visits. Similarly, pastoral care for the dying elderly has become somewhat controversial among adult children who may not appreciate it as much as their parents. Opting for "celebration of life" events instead of traditional funerals in an effort to circumvent all negative connotations around the unspoken word "death" means that the local pastor may be the last person to find out that one of his shut-ins has just died.

Jesus promises much of this in the latter days (Matt 24:10–12). But the bottom line is that there is less and less secular attraction for becoming or remaining a pastor. To the contrary, there are lots of temptations to abandon the ministry. We are wise never to forget that when you are faithful, the devil is intimidated by you! He wishes that you would abandon your post.

Yet pastors have not only been called to where they presently serve but have been given all that they need for success in their call. When that success is invisible to your eyes, just remember the stories of your predecessors like Job or even Jesus. Their victories were clear and certain though shrouded in suffering, sweat, and blood. After all, it is the cross, despised by the world and dismissed as foolish (1 Cor 1:18), that characterizes Christian ministry. What the wisdom of the world fails to grasp is that Jesus' invitation to pick up our crosses and follow him (Matt 16:24) isn't nihilistic or defeatist. Rather, it is nothing less than a celebratory response to the victory chant of the triumphant church of heaven.

From an earthly perspective, ministry is a waste of time at best, and criminal at worst, in societies that deny sin's existence. Still we fight on the winning side, despite all appearances to the contrary. Moreover, we lack nothing as we parade God's armor and operate his efficacious weapons, however unpopular they may be. The armor suffices against the flaming darts of the devil, and the gospel serves as the antidote against any evil infection to which we may be exposed.

Usually we don't even realize the power to which we have access in the armor that we wear and weapons that we handle. Whether we believe it or not, we are often like David before Goliath, equipped with only one small pebble. One small word of God is like that pebble, which topples over our enemies because God is the power behind it. Whether it be zealously slung from the tongue of a preacher, silently flung from the hands folded in prayer, or gently tossed alongside a piece of bread and chalice of wine during a pastoral visit, the "word of God is quick, and powerful" (Heb 4:12

KJV). "So shall my word be that goes out from my mouth; it shall not return to me empty, but it shall accomplish that which I purpose, and shall succeed in the thing for which I sent it" (Isa 55:11).

To make matters even better, angels are always present at the key moments of salvation history. They arrive with might and power, as at that first Easter, rolling away the massive boulder and hurling the guards onto their faces with an earthquake (Matt 28:2). They appear in the lion's den, shutting the mouths of dangerous beasts. Pastors minister at the mouths of various tombs. They silence the voices of demons with their Christ-centered words of advice and prayerful wisdom. Through their ministry, the same risen Christ is once again present with his powerful host of angels, "and the gates of hell shall not prevail against it" (Matt 16:18).

The Lord's Word as Our Sword

Every sermon rattles the soul with the power of God whenever it accurately divides the word of truth. The law cuts. The gospel cures. Like St. George piercing the evil dragon with a spear, the old self is put to death with a cutting blade, which convicts the heart of sin. Following God's rebukes are consoling words of peace—God's forgiveness in Jesus Christ—as a new self emerges and arises to live before God in righteousness and purity of life. But some pastors seem to treat preaching as a motivational speech or a chance to share some helpful advice to live by. If we only believed that we were soldiers surrounded by an unconquerable army, with sharpened tongues as our chief spiritual weapon, we would better appreciate that the command to stay alert at our posts carries a word of encouragement to those who have "no need to be ashamed, rightly handling the word of truth" (2 Tim 2:15) as they "proclaim the gospel to the whole creation" (Mark 16:15).

There are times and seasons in our ministries when we do not feel fulfilled. It is as if the week, month, or year was totally unproductive and our position at the church seems like a big mistake. When you don't think that you or your message matters as much as it once did, you are more likely not to speak boldly nor confess clearly. The demons love when our mouths are shut so that *they* can be heard instead. Our silence is broken by demonic voices that utter worldly points of view and opinions through media and popular culture. Yet every time we contradict falsehood with the truth, we swing the sword of the Spirit. Whenever we believe that our confession and defense of the one holy and apostolic church matters, we have once again extinguished the flaming darts of the devil with the shield of faith.

When I have offered instruction on the ministry of deliverance, I warn eager young pastors that no one should go looking for quarrels with the demonic hordes. Ghost-buster clergy looking to zap demons with their newfound knowledge will likely get a beating. Just as the sheep are not found far from the shepherd, the shepherd is to stay close by to the Chief Shepherd and remain cautious about wandering into unknown territory, which may not have the Lord's mandate or blessing.

I knew a pastor who was anxious for the opportunity to exorcize a demon. He read books, enrolled in seminars, emailed, and called me up with all sorts of speculative questions. Months later I heard that he had left the ministry. He got his chance to perform, but something went wrong. He went running away from the parish in disillusionment.

When we practice ministry in our own power, in accordance with our own wisdom and in our own stead, we will always fall on our face. A pastor doesn't go looking for the devil, but he doesn't run from him either. Pastors serving under the sign of our Lord's holy cross don't sleep but stand guard. They do not leave their posts when the going gets tough. Instead, "be watchful, stand firm in the faith" (1 Cor 16:13).

Demons are devoted to frightening you and making you run. I have learned that the best way to keep calm during an exorcism and to remain unintimidated by the monstrous perversions in plain sight is to just close my eyes and pray. When they speak, you silence and rebuke them, allowing God's wonderful word and powerful voice to drown out the devil's vociferous utterances and malicious noise.

Whether the battle seems intense or feels rather mundane, the evil one is hard at work. Yet in every spiritual battle in your ministry, you are not alone. Behind you stands a legion of holy angels, outnumbering any evil foes. And they are not at all frightened. They are calm, at peace, and joyful. They support you in your calling.

When we engage in spiritual battle, we must rely on God as our strength. The Holy Spirit ensures it. Have you ever wondered why you often preach best when you are struggling with personal concerns? Our suffering keeps our eyes—and tongues—fixed on "Jesus, the founder and per-fecter of our faith" (Heb 12:2).

When possible, fast before the (rare) occasion of addressing an outright demon possession. Both simple prayer and sincere fasting do more damage to the devils' armies than all the rites of exorcism combined. Why? Because prayer is driven by need. It acknowledges that we are unable to achieve anything on our own. Fasting makes us feel weak instead of strong. Nobody feels happy, healthy, or confident on an empty stomach. It's harder to fight on your own. Due to the tight-knit relation-ship between the body and soul, feeling physically unsatisfied evokes a parallel phenomenon of which we may often be unaware: our spiritual emptiness apart from Christ. This is good. Every pastoral act is then fulfilled in Jesus alone. His presence is our bread. His spirit is our strength.

Soldiers are trained to clean their gear after battle in preparing for the next clash as they fight on behalf of those they seek to protect. Caring for God's equipment goes hand in hand with caring for oneself. Pastors clean their kit when they refresh themselves by prayerfully meditating upon the word of God and repeatedly drinking from the cup of the Lord's salvation (Ps 116:13). Such acts of

Christian piety and devotion strengthen our feeble knees in our standing (Heb 12:12) so that we can help steady those of others.

CHAPTER 6

Demonic Temptations in Ministry

The Lord Almighty grant us a quiet night
and peace at the last.
—Opening Sentence of Compline

UNFORTUNATELY, WE DON'T GET TO CHOOSE our battles nor when they occur. It wasn't an accident that Jesus' temptation in the desert immediately followed his baptism in the Jordan. Yet angels support us in all of our spiritual battlefields, lifting up our wearied souls.

Consider how they ministered to Jesus during his agonizing forty days in the desert. He must have felt that he was alone in the world, save for the company of his archenemy. And the deceiver knows all the tricks in the book—how to wear us down. We shouldn't be surprised to hear how tired Jesus was after his incredible fast and the devil's spiritual assaults. The devil knew that if he was going to defeat our Lord, it would be when Jesus was at his physically and emotionally most vulnerable. The devil, as a master of a thousand arts, is incomparably clever and crafty. His temptations are so individualized that it might seem at times as if only you and he exist.

Yet it's all lies, from the "father of lies" (John 8:44). When we believe that from the start, we've already won half the battle. For in your battlefield, you aren't alone. You are surrounded by angels. They are there to encourage, help, and even intervene.

The great deceiver's temptations aren't as simple as we often think. The three temptations that Jesus endured when he fought the devil in the desert at the beginning of his ministry had less to do with satisfying his own needs than with the needs of those he had come to serve and save. They were tempting because they targeted his love for humankind.

Russian author Fyodor Dostoevsky explores the complexity of our Lord's temptation in the desert in a thought-provoking way: Did Satan's challenge for him to turn stones into bread simply appeal to a carnal necessity? The struggle centered on Jesus' care and concern for other people—he was tempted to solve the temporal problem of world hunger over the spiritual and eternal hunger of souls.[21]

Similarly, in the second temptation, Satan plays with Jesus' charitable character. The top of the temple was visible to everyone. What better place to prove to the world that Jesus was the almighty promised Messiah? Seeing is believing, right? Then people would follow him. Amazing the world with a miracle was the kindest thing he could possibly do, wasn't it?

Finally, the devil tempted Jesus with the possession of all earthly authority. Was our Lord tempted by personal power? Not likely. But by love, yes. Consider all the great things that could happen if the wisest, most compassionate, and just man ever didn't die nor ascend into heaven but remained on the earth, governing as its perfect ruler. It would be heaven on earth, right? What better candidate for king? Wouldn't it be selfish for Jesus to decline the offer? Clearly, Jesus did not want to go to the cross in the first place (Luke 22:42)—the experience in the desert was only a tiny foretaste of the scorching trials of Calvary.

All these temptations were alluring not only because they were intended to deflect our Lord from his humble path toward the cross, a vocation of servanthood and suffering, but also because he could have done a lot of good for others by changing goals. The internal battle of our great High Priest involved tossing aside his human emotions, desires, and intuitions, no matter how pure they were, in order to be sacrificed for us and our salvation in Jerusalem.

Satan knew this, and was he afraid. He didn't want his prisoners freed, the gates of hell ripped open, and God's kingdom to come. He didn't want his head crushed (Gen 3:15)! As a Bible thumper of sorts, Lucifer was well-versed in the very Scriptures that he despised. So the devil tried to prevent Jesus from following through on what he came to do by targeting his one potential weak spot: his love for humankind.

We all know what Jesus did, setting the example for the rest of us. Even Jesus used Scripture to counter the evil one: "You shall not put the Lord your God to the test" (Luke 4:12). The temptation was intense. Yet reading the Bible isn't our only strategy. Whenever we hear God speak to us in his word, we speak back to God in prayer. He is eager to hear and answer the prayers of his disheartened children.

The temptation to abandon his messianic mission and the need to fight back with the sword of the Spirit continues right until the end, culminating at the garden of Gethsemane as he "knelt down and prayed, saying, 'Father, if you are willing, remove this cup from me. Nevertheless, not my will, but yours, be done.' And there appeared to him an angel from heaven, strengthening him" (Luke 22:41–43).

That didn't mean the tumultuous temptations were over, but now he had help. "And being in agony he prayed more earnestly; and his sweat became like great drops of blood falling down to the ground" (Luke 22:44). Our Chief Shepherd sets a prescriptive pattern for us under-shepherds. Temptation is fought from our knees with prayer, and prayer is accompanied with pain and suffering. God will never permit us to suffer more than we can handle. "God is faithful, and he will not let you be tempted beyond your ability, but with the temptation he will also provide the way of escape, that you may be able to endure it" (1 Cor 10:13). Even though the load may seem too heavy to carry at times, Jesus is right there carrying it for us. Even though you may believe the lie that there is no way out, the holy angels are right beside you, ministering to you as they did to Jesus.

Now reflect upon some of the most dangerous temptations in your ministry—whether money, sex, power, and so on. These are actually the easy temptations to address since there are explicit Bible passages that identify and convict us of these sins. Our consciences clearly illuminate our stumbling in these regards, and we rejoice that the Lord forgives us. Then we move on in his grace. But there are other sins and errors that aren't so obvious.

As in the case of Jesus, the devil preys on our love and zeal for those we serve. A Bible verse can often be twisted to support just about any pastoral decision that we have already decided feels like the caring thing to do. We are tempted to tell people what they want to hear, not the hard truth, because we feel sorry for them or are simply tired of them bugging us with their questions or problems.

It may be because we are afraid of jeopardizing our reputation as a gentle and kind pastor or, even worse, being antagonized by others though we were simply trying to "hold firm to the trustworthy word as taught ... to give instruction in sound doctrine and also to rebuke those who contradict it" (Titus 1:9). Although intellectually we know that it is his message and that we are simply the messengers, our hearts dread those difficult conversations when we need to address the flawed decisions, beliefs, or behaviors of our parishioners.

We faithful shepherds fear the accusations that arise during those uncomfortable conversations: "It's none of your business," "You are being judgmental," or "The church is so legalistic." One parishioner, who defended her lack of faithful church attendance by pronouncing that she did her own church at home, dismissed my concerns about her spiritual life as old-fashioned opinions. But true love does not simply tolerate people's bad choices. It's part of the pastor's job to dissuade people from making decisions that hurt themselves and others. Although the Scriptures advise that "every person be quick to hear, slow to speak" (Jas 1:19), this can be used erroneously as an excuse to avoid speaking the truth in love.

As a military chaplain and officer, I was expected to be honest and transparent when addressing deficient behavior or a questionable decision made by the troops. The military is not only efficient, it recognizes the severe consequences on others' welfare when we tiptoe around the truth or avoid making tough decisions when they are necessary.

Thankfully, Christ didn't ask permission from us when he chose to die for us on the cross. God made an executive decision, and he made it out of love. Sometimes pastors need to do so too. When we are not bold preachers of the full counsel of God and we let our personal feelings and intuitions get in the way of godly decision-making, we neglect to carry out the tasks assigned to us by the Lord.

Pastoral Decision-Making: Too Active

The tough temptations don't just involve being too passive. Sometimes we want to be overly active— to get too involved in people's lives due to the genuine desire to help them.

Jesus was tempted to do things when it wasn't his time to do them. Instead he knew he needed to just wait and be passive. All he did was speak the word. That's it.

For us, by lacking patience, neglecting to cling to the promises of God and forgetting in whose stead we stand, we can unintentionally create dependency from our parishioners upon us. In those cases, we become their savior instead of leaving that to Christ. They end up entrusting all their complex personal problems into our hands—financial, marital, mental—as opposed to the Lord's.

Clearly, pastors carry the burdens of the congregations. This yoke is symbolized by the clerical collars and liturgical stoles that many wear (see image above). But still, it is actually the person of Christ upon whom we cast all of our burdens (1 Pet 5:7). When we don't realize that we have given into the temptation to get too involved in the lives of our parishioners, we allow ourselves to be taken advantage of, and we do them a disservice by depriving them of having faith in God. Nobody is better off.

It takes more courage to empower others to take responsibility for their problems than to do it for them. I have found that people suffering from substance addiction will often seek freedom from their spiritual affliction, yet without a real desire to be bound to Christ. After all, everyone has a master. We are either slaves to Satan or servants of Christ. But many people behave as if they want freedom from both, which is neither possible nor desirable.

True repentance involves sincere confession of this miserable state. Ultimately, only the Holy Spirit can create that heart condition in our people. Pastors need to be patient, take a step back, and simply pray. Sometimes they even need to shake the dust off of their feet (Matt 10:14) and break with people, not because they are self-righteous or impatient, but because some situations need to get worse before they can get better. As heart wrenching as it is, leaving them alone may help them see how dire their needs are. This too is spiritual warfare, and this too is love. Sometimes we need to hand people over to Satan—that is, let them live without biblical counsel—for a season (1 Cor 5:5). As painful as it is to watch, we do so in hope: God hasn't left or forsaken them (Deut 31:6).

I once performed an exorcism on a nominal Christian haunted by years of demonic possession. He was very grateful for my service. Freed from the demons that harassed him so terribly, he could sleep better. He stopped gnashing his teeth at night. He felt more at peace.

As is my custom, I counseled him to recommence a life of prayer and deeper devotion, Bible study, and church attendance and participation in the worship life of a local Christian community. However, he didn't think he was ready for any of that. The next time he visited me to receive deliverance from demonic entities, I didn't do it. It was a painful pastoral decision. He wanted me to pray for him and rebuke the devil on his behalf, but he wasn't willing to do any of it himself. He wouldn't own his problem and take responsibility for his spiritual state. And, so, the demons remained.

I happened to be working alongside a medical doctor on that case. Incidentally, this medical professional had become a believer through the supernatural phenomenon that he witnessed pertaining to this shared client. When I turned away the man that day, the doctor was concerned that our patient was unsafe to drive home, since he was at least partially under the control of this demonic influence and not in entire control of his faculties. I chose to entrust him to the Lord.

I didn't sleep that well that night, wondering if he would be physically injured and if it would be my fault. It turned out that our patient didn't sleep either, since he called me a couple of days later confessing that he had survived some of the worst days of his life. He begged to see me again, saying, "I am ready now." He was ready to say "no" to the beast; ready to face—to own—his problem. Yet I still made him make the plans. Then, together, he and I organized a meeting at a local church for a second exorcism.

Letting Go of Others

A lot of people ignore the pastor's advice. Sadly, their lives get worse. Some are so clearly hostages to sin or victims of spiritual abuse that, if you are like me, you get tempted to want to live their lives for them, finding ways to babysit them so that you don't need to keep cleaning up their mess. "If only they had listened to us," we sigh. To make matters worse, as soon as one problem is resolved in the life of a distressed parishioner, a whole new slew of worse problems creeps over the horizon. Unless we let our people take responsibility for their own issues, obliging them to bring their problems and sins to God their Father themselves, we are sure to burn out with compassion fatigue. We need to let go of others, carefully. Don't drop them on the ground, but hand them over to Jesus, prayerfully and transparently—in open discussion with your parishioner—from your caring hand to Christ's.

If we don't, we take the undesirable outcomes of our parishioner's crisis personally. We inadvertently bring upon ourselves unnecessary stress and unhealth of all kinds. We convince ourselves that this is the cost of discipleship. But really, our suffering is often caused by our own bad decisions. Instead of "casting all your anxieties upon [Christ], because he cares for you" (1 Pet 5:7)—and letting others do the same!—we give into the temptation to handle things ourselves.

If we had only listened to our Master, it would have been different. We are shepherds, but Jesus is the Chief Shepherd. He loves our people more than we do. He can, and does, clean up their messes in his time. And he also cleans up ours. He "came not to be served but to serve, and to give his life as a ransom for many" (Mark 10:45).

Because God doesn't forsake his sheep, neither do their pastors obviously. After all, pastors are fathers of families, and it's natural at times to get frustrated with your kids' decisions. Yet sometimes our choices need to contradict our instincts. And like God our heavenly Father in the parable of the prodigal son, we need to be willing to abandon our concerns at the foot of Christ's cross, giving them into the outstretched arms of our Lord. When pastors are patient with worrisome members who don't behave in the ways that they ought, they exhibit mature trust in God's providence and that his grace is sufficient (2 Cor 12:9).

Patience goes both ways. Congregations sometimes need to endure the weaknesses of their minister for a season. Spiritual growth in one part of our life may not necessarily be as evident in another. A young, headstrong pastor who is theologically mature may lack compassion when it comes to less academically astute believers. Even sincere pastors trying their best to father their spiritual families can fall into the sin of becoming domineering.

They don't realize that they are acting in hurtful and abusive ways, victimizing their flock. Such tendencies and temptations can be more readily avoided by directing our eyes away from ourselves and toward Christ's cross for help and guidance. It's difficult to be blind to our faults when gazing upon perfection and its willful embodiment in self-sacrifice. A wise and experienced bishop or ecclesiastical supervisor can help pastors see these deficiencies more clearly and find ways of reestablishing peace within their congregations. I have found that most pastors are open to these processes, since they legitimately want to serve their flock. But knowing how to move forward after messing up isn't as intuitive.

Repentance precedes a daily examination and confession of all the sins that we have committed against our pastoral office, then turning to our heavenly Father for help and guidance. Sometimes the laity are the best preachers to pastors in these moments. Although Nathan is subordinate to the king, he boldly rebukes David for failing to acknowledge his own sins of adultery and murder (2 Sam 12). Sometimes it takes a lamb to correct the shepherd. Pastors need to hear the same words of both law and gospel that they share with others.

Only in the divine covenant of God with human-kind can reconciliation within a hurting congregation be fostered. The word of God always heals the humbled hearts of broken people.

For when our choices are not driven by trust in God and obedience to his word, we be governed instead by workaholism or laziness, egoism or apathy, tendencies to be abused or to abuse depending on our personalities. Instead, like the father in the parable (Luke 15:11–32) and like the angels in heaven, we are expected to take a step back and observe from a distance while we eagerly anticipate their repentant return. Most of all, we pray, since we ultimately can do nothing but trust in God.

Welcoming Suffering

We are sure to suffer for our God-pleasing choices. We will suffer because of others. It is the unavoidable consequence of being in close proximity to our parishioners as loving caregivers. Their hurt is contagious.

Pastors don't flee from suffering. They embrace it. Though tempted to drop our cross and follow the easiest, least painful, and most self-fulfilling way, the Holy Spirit keeps us on the straight and narrow path to Golgotha in our spiritual Jerusalems. Servanthood includes suffering. "Beloved, do not be surprised at the fiery trial when it comes upon you to test you, as though something strange were happening to you. But rejoice insofar as you share Christ's sufferings, that you may also rejoice and be glad when his glory is revealed" (1 Pet 4:12–13). Picking up our crosses and following Jesus is good—though, admittedly, the beauty is hidden therein.

Framing can change our perception. It's like how a gifted photographer can take an ordinary object and transform it into something lovely: when framed carefully in the lens, what seemed mundane is revealed to be extraordinary and noteworthy. Even an ugly object, viewed through the lens in a certain way, can become beautiful. A dull rock or a battered old tree becomes an intriguing artwork, edifying to mind and soul. So too our lives, when penetrated by sadness, hurt, and anxiety, appear dark and gloomy at first glance. But when framed by the cross, our bleak moments of suffering are transformed into glorious masterpieces, wonderful and meaningful. When we view our lives through a lens of hope, we look with the eyes of Jesus. "Not only that, but we rejoice in our sufferings, knowing that suffering produces endurance, and endurance produces character, and character produces hope, and hope does not put us to shame, because God's love has been poured into our hearts through the Holy Spirit who has been given to us" (Rom 5:3–5).

We need to trust God's word alone to interpret our experiences and make sense of the demonic trials we endure. "In your light do we see light" (Ps 36:9). Evaluating our ministries and interactions with people according to the results we observe is dangerous. The devil can mimic victory. False churches and cults often boast the biggest assemblies. The occult promises personal gains and even supernatural abilities, such as fortune telling or voodoo. False teaching attracts many followers. When we evaluate according to our own intuitions, we suffer unnecessarily with self-inflicted pain. We needlessly bear the compounded weight of our sin when we fail to recognize the liberty gained at the cross.

Those involved in the ministry of deliverance will testify that in exorcisms, things are not always as they appear. When demons talk, they will give you words that you want to hear. They may even say things to make you feel more self-confident in order to sidetrack you from Jesus as your only hope and confidence. They are liars. They are tricksters. A demon may even pretend to have left the one that he inhabits, duping the pastor into thinking certain techniques, rites, and rituals work better than others. Demons want to tempt you to rely upon your own expertise instead of on God's word. This is why there is no substitute for simple prayer and unfaltering trust in God's will being done despite any observable success. Victory can never be determined simply by what we see, feel, or experience.

Pastors who suffer for doing the right thing will often have worse lives and smaller churches versus those who cater to people's spiritual appetites and distort the gospel. So, too, prosperity-gospel preachers err by insisting that a successful prayer is the one that achieves that for which it has asked. I once knew a woman from whom I continually exorcized demons and who shared my heart-wrenching discouragement over failing to keep the demons out.[22] I felt like a terrible and useless pastor, tediously searching for the perfect piece of equipment in the pastor's toolbox and coming up empty handed. Yet, in hindsight, I've realized that these demonic episodes kept her coming back to church, Sunday after Sunday. As insane as it sounds, demon possession kept her grounded in faith in Jesus. How many people get their prayer answered as they wished, only to never again find a reason to return to the house of God? Like nine out of the ten lepers, when their prayer gets answered and their petitions cease, so do their thanks (Luke 17:11–19). Miracles don't create faith. Consider the villagers who beg Jesus to depart from them after they witness his casting of demons into the swine (Mark 5:17). Suffering keeps us centered on Christ.

Satanic attacks offer us a chance to reflect upon the cross. When my children have a night terror, I tell them, "Fart in the devil's face—that will chase him away." Then I tell them to say the Lord's Prayer. God's children don't need to be afraid of anything! The devil feeds on fear; "perfect love casts out fear" (1 John 4:18). Without belittling the devil's dangerous influence, we also must avoid taking him too seriously. Otherwise, we let his lies obstruct the light of Christ's joy.

Often it can feel like the straight and narrow road is the one that leads to Hades due to the hellfire that we encounter. In those moments, remember that God is in the depths of Sheol (Ps 139:8). It's a great mystery, to be sure: God is present even in the place that we would think him absent, the darkness of hell. Yet isn't this what Good Friday is all about? Jesus' best expression of love culminates in his presence within the uttermost darkness. The paradox isn't meant to tease our brain but to give us great comfort in the midst of our personal hellish struggles. Moreover, his physical descent into hell demonstrates that he even rules there in victory and power, since nothing can separate us from his love (Rom 8:35–39). For even the devil is subjected to him as an inadvertent tool and unwilling servant. Still all things must answer to God as the king of the universe. For "I am convinced that he is able to guard until that day what has been entrusted to me" (2 Tim 1:12). And God remains the master of all the seemingly out-of-control parts of our ministries.

SUFFERING SERVANTS VERSUS ABUSED VICTIMS

There is a fine line between turning the other cheek, sacrificing ourselves for others (Matt 5:39–42), and getting abused or being taken advantage of by those that we are trying to help.

All Christians experience this within their various vocations. The devil tempts each one to desert their posts or neglect their duties. The marriage is no longer going well? Satan shouts: "Leave!" Yet his voice isn't always as obvious to discern. The parish life is no longer going well? The devil *whispers*: "Leave."

Just as maximizing success in business may create the temptation to compromise on ethics, so too pastors are tempted to compromise God's word and scriptural doctrine in order to placate others. Again, that crafty serpent uses even the word of God to do it. He did it with Jesus and is sure to do it with us—twisting God's word to satisfy what our "itching ears" want to hear (2 Tim 4:3) and what our bleeding hearts want to feel.

No wonder Jesus welcomed the help of angels while recovering from his temptations in the desert and enduring them at Gethsemane. And Jesus could tackle evil alone. We can't. Yet just as angels supported him, they support us. We cannot see them, but they are there.

When we do allow angels to strengthen us and care for us, we become more effective caregivers to others, equipped with true wisdom from above. Remembering in whose company we work, we are more apt to carefully apply the holy Scriptures to the unique situations that we encounter—being angels to others by rightly distinguishing the rebukes of the law from the comfort of the gospel. We act as holy angels.

The word "holy" is a difficult one to unpack. It doesn't simply imply the opposite of evil. It involves the notion of separation from that which is common. When Uzzah tried to steady the ark of the covenant, he accidentally touched it and suffered death (2 Sam 6:1–7). He wasn't likely punished for some rebellious act, but he suffered the consequences of a clumsy mistake. Our mistakes, too, can have deadly consequences. Handling God's holy gifts requires focused energy and deliberation. Like a doctor performing surgery, we must take great care. Our unintentional errors and poor decisions can have genuinely hurtful, though forgivable, consequences for ourselves and others.

Careful caregiving means that we become less disposed to pass quickly through the hearing of a Christian brother's or sister's confession of sin without offering any further spiritual guidance after declaring their reconciliation with God in Christ. Sometimes we listen too much and do too little. We don't want to give bad advice informed by worldly wisdom, so we nod our heads without offering any truly applicable word from Scripture. At other times we listen too little and do too much. We assume we know what needs to be done to fix a situation. Then, in retrospect, we discover that we didn't have an accurate pulse on the situation. Both are motivated by love, yet both are misdirected.

Pastors aren't perfect. Even though they act in the stead and by the command of Christ, they aren't Jesus. When pastors humbly acknowledge this truth in word and deed, parishioners' admiration for the pastoral office isn't diminished. To the contrary! And repenting of sins and confessing our weaknesses reminds us humans that the pastoral office supersedes every individual who fills it. For Christ is its content, power, and authority. When we esteem the office of the holy ministry, we esteem the One who is its source and life.

When pastors and people are honest with one another about human limitations and realistic expectations, they act as angels to one another. Every load is lighter when carried by more than one. Pastors are accustomed to carrying the loads of others, and so they are often less inclined to permit others to return the service.

Even the almighty Son of God, who is perfectly holy and good, welcomed the help of ministering spirits after his wrestling match with Satan. Pastors and their people who have recovered well from their respective battles have usually learned some tough lessons. But that puts them in the best shape to help others face their own battles (Eph 4:12) and confront their own demons.

Self-Care: Not Optional

Even Jesus needed some time to recuperate after his battle with the evil one. He also regularly took time alone in prayer, setting an example for all church workers. Yet it remains a common problem among clergy and helping professionals. They spend so much time occupied in the lives of others that they neglect to ensure that they are staying healthy in body, mind, and soul themselves. Especially after those intense battles we undergo in parish life, a recovery period is highly recommended. Those witnessing a successful exorcism may feel euphoric afterward, as they celebrate the mighty acts of their Maker. But that sentiment is speedily followed by intense physical exhaustion. Sometimes, the demon may begin harassing the clergy out of spite. That is just some of the predictable collateral damage of participation in the ministry of deliverance. Because pastoral care implicates body, mind, and soul, those who practice it need an opportunity to recuperate from their own wounds and also from the impact that the suffering of others has had on themselves. Counselors are required to take time between clients—they don't jump immediately from one case to another. Yet clergy may have a more difficult time identifying that need until it's too late. For Christians and pastors, self-care isn't about getting more time for self. It's permitting ourselves to be cared for by Jesus and the angels. In other words, "Christ care."

Positive Christian Thinking

Without the maintenance of a healthy spirituality—which is difficult to have when you are burning out due to lack of self-care!—we Christians can become overly negative when we should be rejoicing (Phil 4:4). Jesus' Beatitudes tell us that we are blessed when we suffer. A church or ministry that suffers is one that the devil has deemed worthy of persecution. Even in the darkest episodes of our congregational histories, the Lord has been orchestrating the events of our lives toward his greater good. So he says, "Do not be anxious about anything" (Phil 4:6).

Sometimes we let our feelings take over. Our reasoning grows clouded. But just because we are sinners, we aren't required to approach the future with doom and gloom. We are also saints. That itself merits rejoicing. As God's holy ones, we are encircled by the company of other holy ones— the angels—and are surrounded with their joy. Christians are allowed to be positive without denying the prominence of sin in the world. Christian cheerfulness is the fruit of joy. And joy—which stays afloat, despite the ups and downs of our feelings—presumes an outlook on life that rests on the goodness of God's creation and his sovereign and merciful reign over it. The "joy of the LORD is your strength" (Neh 8:10).

Many people who struggle with mental illness spend too much time thinking about themselves and their problems. This includes pastors. If you can get them outside of themselves and focused on others, leading them away from introspective reflection to some servant projects or volunteer work, they find not only purpose and meaning but all sorts of previously hidden beauties in life. One acquaintance of mine was highly disdainful and judgmental of others. He was introverted and didn't like talking with people. But when I finally got him to speak with others in a way that demonstrated sincere interest in their lives, he was able to see their admirable qualities, that they too had problems and feelings along with interesting stories to tell. With this realization he was less inclined to view them in a negative light. His thinking shifted from despising others to finding ways to help them.

When we pastors approach our lives and ministries with a positive outlook, not denying our sinfulness and limitations but with healthy trust that God's goodness can never be overcome by our dire circumstances, the counsel that we offer to others will also follow suit.

A church leader once asked me to advise on a spiritual situation that had affected a small American town. A murder had occurred in a house where occult rituals had allegedly taken place. The neighbors thought it was cursed and had it condemned by the town. Yet strange and devilish activity attached to a particular item at the house continued terrorizing the community. They wanted closure. I advised them to burn and bury the object in a field, praying a short prayer addressing the demonic activity. Then I told them to proceed with a hymn sing at the site without any further mention of the frightening story (Phil 4:8). The community used this traumatic experience as an opportunity to unite in Christ-centered worship, praising God for the wonders of creation and his abundant mercies. By using this tragedy as a chance to focus on positive truths about God, the devil became an ironic catalyst to an increase of faith in God and love between one another.

Demons still are instruments of God, even though they are rebellious servants that have lost their way. Their attitudes can be contagious if we aren't careful. Yet whenever negative things direct our eyes back to Jesus, from darkness to light, those creatures are put to good use again. When we allow God to use the specific temptations that we face in our pastoral vocation for the greater good, we remain victors over them in Christ.

CHAPTER 7

Demonic Games and Mental Health

Blessed are You, O Lord our God,
king of the universe, who led Your people Israel
by a pillar of cloud by day and a pillar of fire
by night. Enlighten our darkness by the light
of Your Christ; may His Word be a lamp
to our feet and a light to our path;
for You are merciful, and You love
Your whole creation and we, Your creatures,
glorify You, Father, Son and Holy Spirit.
—Thanksgiving for Light, from Evening Prayer

THE WAR IS OVER—THE DEVIL AND HIS EVIL minions have been defeated by our Lord Jesus Christ's cross at Calvary—yet the battle continues.

Christians live between the times. Christ has come. Christ will come again. Although the armies of the evil one are defeated, persistent attacks by these sore losers continue. Their tyranny often pivots on creative attempts to convince the church that they still have power. Her angelic leaders—clergy—are targeted to a greater degree than others. In accordance with his divine wisdom and sovereign plan for humankind, God Almighty permits demons this freedom until the parousia, when "the great dragon" and "ancient serpent" (Rev 12:9) will forever be cast away.

As a pastor, I find that one of the church's most meaningful services is the Easter vigil on Holy Saturday. The service is mainly spoken. With interior lights dimmed—a single candle illuminating the sacred space—words are proclaimed that convey historical and objective truth. You can barely see the liturgist. You hear God's word in the shadows. After all, "the light shines in the darkness, and the darkness has not overcome it" (John 1:5).

Because it interrupts our holiday weekend, and many Christians feel that they have spent enough time in church during Holy Week, the vigil is often poorly attended. And so a faithful few and a crowd of angels celebrate the empty grave and resurrection even before the sunrise of Easter. Our risen Lord physically descended into hell, as we confess in the Apostles' Creed, not to suffer more torment and abuse but to proclaim his victory and free the prisoners of Hades. Jesus crashes the devil's premature victory party.

The service consists of a series of Old Testament readings of divine deliverance, all of them fore-shadowing Jesus' means of delivering us from evil today.[23] He is proclaimed as the light who enters the darkness as a single candle, penetrating the darkness of the dimly lit room, which is carried to the altar and placed under the cross. There is no light without sacrifice. "The LORD is God, and he has made his light to shine upon us. Bind the festal sacrifice with cords, up to the horns of the altar!" (Ps 118:27).

The Easter vigil is not my favorite service, but the one I need the most. It's the one that stands out for me, sandwiched between the mournful sounds of Good Friday and the joyous trumpet blasts of Easter. It doesn't provide any space for romanticism, idealism, or sentimentalism. In its courageous commitment to pronouncing the glo-rious light of Christ, it refuses to deny the exis-tence of darkness. It dismantles any perfectionism or unrealistic expectations for ministry. It presumes that sin, suffering, and turmoil continue to surround the lives of the redeemed and sanctified. Yet there is light, and this light is never extinguished.

The light illumines the darkness, and yet the sanctuary remains dark. It symbolizes our own unsettling existence between contrasting spiritual dimensions. On the last day, we will experience victory over the forces of hell. In the meantime, we live in paradox. God calls us saints, but we feel only our sin. We are holy, yet we suffer. We reconcile these conflicting realities by faith. We believe. "For now we see through a glass, darkly; but then face to face" (1 Cor 13:12 KJV).

Our eyes behold a bloody battle on Good Friday. We want to flee to Easter. Instead, we should linger. For it is precisely in the passion of Christ that we encounter victory. Our own experiences are a microcosm of Christ's experience: our victories are often hidden, too. Pastors fight on the front line. We observe the war from a very limited vantage point. Angels see it from an elevated perspective. They know we need not worry about the outcome. When we approach our ministry from this heavenly viewpoint, we have no reason to fear.

The demons are hard at work in spite of their defeat. They know that their time is short and so they seek to take as many souls as they can to hell. The battle is manifested within the hearts and lives of our members and ourselves. As pastors, the devil preys on our unhappiness, discontent, and doubts. Yet we have not been left without strategies to address each one of these demonic games.

THE FATHER OF LIES

The devil wants to kill you—but he can't. He can't actually physically injure Christians. But he can lie to them. Incidentally, this is his fiercest weapon. Words are powerful. They have the ability to hurt or heal. God creates with his true and living word; the devil demolishes with his. This "father of lies" (John 8:44) wants us to doubt God's promises, just as Adam and Eve did: "Did God actually say?" (Gen 3:1). He tries to lead us away from the entire truth with his manipulation—and he uses partial truths to do so.

All lies are manipulations of the truth, and that is precisely why they are so compelling and believable. When we believe the devil's distortions of the truth, our perception of reality becomes skewed. Without realizing it, we judge spiritual matters like unbelievers. We suffer from spiritual myopia. The devil points to a true fact—a sin over which we ought to feel guilt. But then he twists it, using that fact to tell us a partial truth. He excludes the forgiveness of sins. He distracts us from the whole truth with other falsehoods, such as that God is unloving or lacks compassion. When we listen to his voice, which can sound very reasonable at times, we fall into his snare. Satan takes a little bit of truth and twists it, trying to get us to despair, as he did with Judas.

This is why pastors shouldn't trust their eyes, feelings, and personal experiences when assessing the success of their ministries. God's word alone must remain our filter in deciphering the meaning of life's events; it must be the principal instrument through which we view our world.

The devil is highly skilled at confirming the negative things we think about ourselves. He blows them out of proportion in hopes that they may eclipse the cross of Jesus. He misuses our consciences and accuses us of being a bad pastor, parent, or person. He is a master at preaching the law of God, showing us all the ways that we break the Ten Commandments. And the mirror of God's law does reveal our spiritual ugliness—but it's only half the story. God uses that mirror to chase us to Christ, whose spiritual beauty is reflected onto us. The devil does all he can to keep us at the mirror. Peter was as guilty as Judas, but he refused to give up faith in redemption. Both betrayed the Lord, both sinned, but only one believed in a greater, more important truth: the gospel.

I have met countless disillusioned pastors who have believed the lie that the ministry is theirs. They are unable to "bless those who curse you, pray for those who abuse you" (Luke 6:28) because they forget that the rejection that they experience in the ministry isn't directed toward them. When their honest zeal for the ministry doesn't produce the fruits that they had hoped for, they take it personally. Like Job, they are tempted to believe the wisdom of the world as echoed through the well-intended but false ideas of supposed friends. They strive harder than ever to make their ministries prosper, but to no avail. Or they give up trying entirely.

Because our bodies and souls are knit tightly together, such spiritual baggage often has physical consequences. The high achievers burn out. Some spiral into depression. Others experience the effects in more subtle ways. I know of several dispirited clergy who cope by socially isolating themselves. They withdraw or emotionally distance themselves, bemoaning their lack of deep relationships. In both cases, a parallel pattern is exhibited in their relationship with God. Their hearts become distanced from the Lord even while they continue to offer him to others. They become spiritually desensitized, going through the motions of carrying out their pastoral duties while their hearts are distant. Often, no one notices except God and his angels. This includes the fallen angels, who are quick to note the fissures in our spiritual lives so that they can pry at them and wriggle in an extra dose of deceit.

Wounded pastors make great healers, but not while they're bleeding. For others' sake as much as their own, they require self-care. All pastors need to remove themselves occasionally from the spiritual war zone in order to receive directed, spiritual medical attention. A religious retreat can help. A holiday with the family can rejuvenate the spirit. But nothing compares with time alone with Christ.

One of my most memorable ministry experiences was an evening when the police showed up to my residence informing me that a member of mine, with severe psychological issues, had escaped from the psychiatric ward. They feared suicide. Evidently, I was the last one to whom she had spoken. I vividly remembered counseling her the day before: "Don't listen to the voices saying that you have no worth. You are valuable. Christ died for you. God is your life." To this day, I praise God that they found her.

When I visited her at the hospital later, she didn't want me to do much talking, praying, or preaching. She simply asked me for holy Communion. She confided that during her roughest moments of mental crisis, her greatest joy, hope, and help was encountering God's promises in such a tangible and objective way. Her faith fluctuated, as happens to us all. Her heart was unreliable. Her thoughts were scrambled. She found no peace from looking inside of herself. She knew to look outside. She claimed that the Lord's consecrated bread—Jesus' body—was her only stabilizer and reality check. She was truly blessed because she knew that the devil was real and recognized the destruction of which he is capable with his lies. The devil works discreetly in most of our lives so that we do not feel threatened. Lulled by this false sense of security, we put down our weapons and lower our guard. Like the disciples at the garden of Gethsemane, we fall asleep on the job (Matt 26:40). "But stay awake at all times, praying that you may have strength to escape all these things that are going to take place, and to stand before the Son of Man" (Luke 21:36). Or even worse, when he disguises himself as an "angel of light" (2 Cor 11:14), and we believe Satan's partial truths.

Demonic Games involving the Pastor's Family

As the guardians of the Lord's flock, pastors are especially earmarked by the devil. Take out the leader, and you can divide and conquer the team. With his "flaming darts" (Eph 6:16) he targets our weak spots. For many of us it is our families. It's hard to imagine what life on earth was like before the conception of sin. But we do have a glimpse into the garden of Eden through two estates which are still with us today: marriage and the church.

First, regarding the estate of marriage—relationships between people—God made man and woman as two beautiful but different ways of existing as human beings. Pre-fall, this first husband and wife dwelt in a complementary relationship of reciprocal support and service, loving and cherishing one another with the glad goal of populating God's kingdom with children.

Second, regarding the church—relationships between God and humankind—the first pastor and congregation are found in the figures of Adam and Eve. Adam proclaimed God's wonders to Eve, who gladly heard them.

It's unsurprising, then, that the devil violently attacks those two estates today with such spite and hatred. Endless friction, selfishness, and competition is manifested between the sexes and also between clergy and congregations. Our relationship with God has been corrupted in every conceivable dimension. The devil's rebellious desire to disrupt the divine order within creation is exhibited by persuading these first two creatures to reject God's word as both good and as the sole authoritative principle in governing human behavior. Alienation from God necessarily results in alienation from one another. Until the day of our Lord's glorious return, Christians remain sinners struggling to survive in this fallen world. We remain vulnerable to demonic assaults on all sides.

Many clergy are also spouses, making them prone to a double onslaught. When the devil pursues pastors, he doesn't only seek to ruin their lives but also the lives of their congregations. The cleverest way of achieving this is by targeting the pastor's marriage and family.

We pastors may be able to tolerate attacks on our congregations and even our own well-being. But when it comes to family, we aren't as prepared. The demons know that their best strategy to weaken humble pastors who love their people does not only involve their responsibilities as caregivers to members. By harassing their spouses and children they have an even stronger offensive line of attack.

Celibate pastors may be spared some of this pain, yet they have siblings and parents who they love dearly as well. Sadly, rampant attacks on our families often become the straw that breaks the camel's back for pastors who can't bear the thought of their loved ones hurting due to their workplace stresses.

Sometimes we see this in congregational crisis. I know pastors' children who perceive themselves as not measuring up to the unrealistic holiness standards set by influential members. Sometimes, it's more deeply spiritual and demonic. The wife or kids just seem to have a tougher time in life. In both scenarios, their suffering embodies the collateral damage of spiritual war against the pastoral ministry. I have heard several pastors who have quit the ministry justify it in the lament, "They went after my family." Every Christian must remember that our truest family isn't an earthly community bound together by genetic codes, but a heavenly one united by the blood of Christ: the church. Whenever I perform a child's baptism, I remind the parents that these little ones are given back to Jesus and that they are only on loan to us in the first place. Something similar can be said at a dedication. Our kids are God's, first and foremost. They are in good hands. We can take comfort in knowing that God loves our families more than we do (Matt 7:11). And he can do more to protect them, too.

In some church cultures, the pastor's family is not allowed to have normal problems like everybody else. When their marriage is struggling, as all marriages do at times, pastors feel like they need to hide it from others. Otherwise, they may be misjudged for not having a handle on their household. Their kids feel like they are constantly in the spotlight or on parade. When they are not outstanding examples of Christian life and faith to other children, eyebrows are raised in judgment. Predictably, some rebel under the pressure. It doesn't take much for us to believe the lie that our kids or marriage is linked to the value of our ministries.

As loving shepherds, we don't want to give people reason to stumble or gossip. But by trying to prevent the display of our personal dirty laundry, we can end up pretending that we have none. This devilish vanity amounts to believing that we are morally superior to others. After all, every family has skeletons in their closets that we will only be fully rid of when we enter our heavenly home one day. In the meantime, being authentic in the ministry assumes a level of honesty that doesn't dwell on our personal problems but doesn't deny them either.

In moments when I feel unworthy to shepherd God's flock and second-guess my call as a pastor, I picture the angels with me. The Angel of angels is there too. They all see me—as the old hymn goes—"just as I am," and they aren't ashamed. They don't question my ministry or personal value. In spite of all they know and see, they stay with me. They know that God doesn't make mistakes. Although they are perfect, they sympathize with my weaknesses. They appreciate how every kind of pain and suffering that a Christian endures is the very means by which the muscles of faith grow and our spiritual lives are kept from becoming stagnant.

Strength is made perfect in weakness (2 Cor 12:9). God gives us and our families a lifetime to prepare us for heaven. And sometimes the cleansing of our souls happens in unexpected ways that contradict our reason and wills. Following Abraham, who offered Isaac as a sacrifice, we obey God, believing in his goodness even when we don't understand. "In this you rejoice, though now for a little while, if necessary, you have been grieved by various trials, so that the tested genuineness of your faith—more precious than gold that perishes though it is tested by fire—may be found to result in praise and glory and honor at the revelation of Jesus Christ" (1 Pet 1:6–7). Yet even in the most heated moments of this burning process, our Lord and his Angel don't abandon us in that fiery furnace. As he was with Shadrach, Meshach, and Abednego, so he is with you. He suffered the fires of hell, sin, and suffering to guide—even carry— you through them all.

When we remember that all that we have is an undeserved gift and that we own nothing—"for we brought nothing into the world, and we cannot take anything out of the world" (1 Tim 6:7)—the shaping of our hearts doesn't seem quite as painful.

The Lie of Demonic "Possession"

We don't actually possess anything. This basic truth that we are not our own can't be understated. It's helpful to remember this when we take credit for or become disheartened over our ministry. It's not ours. We don't even possess our own bodies. We gave up any right to them when we were baptized into Christ. Whenever you are spiritually attacked, recall that you belong to Jesus. Your identity is in him. "Demon possession" is an oxymoron—demons only borrow without asking.

A popular superstition holds that the devil owns certain places, objects, and people. We believe stories that some places are so dark, some objects so cursed, some people so evil that they belong to the devil and that even the most righteous of saints lack adequate protection. But we give the fallen angels far too much credit. They own nothing. They are just creatures like us.

We give Satan the glory that he desperately seeks when we witness his workings within the realm of the paranormal and respond with awe and wonder. The old Adam remains attracted to the dark. We gravitate to horror movies and scary novels that we know do not glorify God nor edify others. Yet the new Adam resists because he is possessed by the Holy Ghost and filled with God's Spirit.

In the aftermath of an exorcism, it is advisable for all occult objects be burned to avoid any further evil use of them and to symbolize our rejection of them. But we must not infer from this practice that they are intrinsically evil. Even the ashes still belong to God. God is sovereign over even hell. "If I make my bed in Sheol, you are there!" (Ps 139:8).

God alone creates. The devil can only abuse. When the devil claims to possess people, he has invaded another man's building. This enemy intruder remains in hiding until he is forced to leave. He needs to be told that he doesn't belong; that he is not welcome; that someone else possesses this place. We all belong to God. "You are not your own, for you were bought with a price" (1 Cor 6:19–20).

In the case of Christians, we have been bought with a price, purchased and won by our Lord's atoning death and innocent blood. Unbelievers still belong to God, but because they don't believe it, they are particularly vulnerable to evil lies. For instance, the devil fuels the notion that your body is yours to do with as you please. When offering care to individuals struggling with suicidal tendencies, I have often used the unusual but compelling argument that suicide is theft. After all, your life doesn't belong to you. It belongs to Jesus. He paid the highest of prices to make you his own dear child. And even though suicide is forgivable, "you shall not put the Lord your God to the test" (Luke 4:12). It may sound like a cliché, but God has a purpose for our lives. Instead of simply telling people that there is meaning to their lives, I also tell them that God is using them to make this world a better place.

Even those who the world undervalues are meaningful divine instruments. They are prayer warriors. A young, hospitalized member of my parish was greatly encouraged when I reminded her of all the extra time she could devote to prayer for others. She began to see the room to which she was confined as her chapel. Consider the remarkable influence of the elderly when they are witnesses to their grandchildren. Euthanasia and assisted suicide selfishly deprives the world of God's work through the elderly, though they may be suffering.

Moreover, it denies God's desire to use all of his people to touch the lives of others. It's unhealthy stewardship. Abandoning the ministry makes a similar error. Your vocation is not yours for the choosing. Your life is not yours for the taking. You do not belong to yourself. After all, Satan's goal is to hinder the Lord's ministry of the word as it is manifested in all Christian vocations. When it comes to pastors, he especially seeks to knock out the ministers of the Lord's word: "Strike the shepherd, and the sheep will be scattered" (Zech 13:7). When pastors are tempted to abandon their call, by neglecting their duties, losing a healthy zeal for service, or even quitting, they need immediate help, prayer, and counsel from their colleagues, more than they may think. It's spiritually serious. And it's not just limited to a personal choice. A pastor's identity crisis has severe repercussions on the congregation and wider Christian church.

Insisting too strongly upon our rights can sever us from our God-given identity and, in so doing, prevents us from joyfully living out our faith within our assigned vocations. God made us. So we are "wonderfully made" (Ps 139:14). God has placed us where we are to serve his magnificent purposes. The devil relentlessly seeks to confuse and twist what God has made good until we put him in his place.

Telling the Devil Who You Belong To

Pastoral care requires patience in leading people to celebrate the truth that we are God's chosen people (Deut 14:2) and to actively contradict the devilish and worldly lies. Certainly, because of sin, we will never experience total satisfaction within any of our vocations. Accordingly, spiritual war happens within each one of our callings. Husbands and wives frequently feud. Hostility in the workplace continues. Yet although examples of unholiness abound, all upright vocations are still good. Their beauty is restored in repentance and the forgiveness of sins. The subtle temptations of the devil to incite us to rebel against and within our stations in life are rebuked by remembering who you are in Christ. The powerful word of God and his holy truth will silence all of these lying voices and still every unsettled soul, "for the word of God is living and active, sharper than any two-edged sword" (Heb 4:12). Though we are weak and fragile "jars of clay" (2 Cor 4:7), we remain mighty and powerful "chosen instruments" of God (Acts 9:15). God has made us who we are and placed us where we are in accordance with his good and holy will.

Katerina was a ninety-five-year-old member suffering with severe dementia. She was totally unresponsive to the voices or visits of family members. I didn't have huge expectations during my pastoral visits, except when it came to our prayer time together. As soon as I concluded with the words of the Our Father, she would join me, mumbling the words in Slovak. She too was a Christian soldier. In spite of everything that she no longer knew, despite any internal spiritual struggles that she was passing through, she hadn't forgotten that she belonged to Jesus. God held her in his hand. And nothing could snatch her out from it (John 10:28). God never forgets his own.

There are difficult times in life when every Christian, including pastors, needs to rebuke demonic entities directly. Though rare, these intense moments require an audible word to halt the harassment: "Be gone, Satan!" Some Christians cross themselves when they feel threatened. This isn't necessarily superstition. When Christians make the sign of the cross, they are retracing the same markings that they received when they were baptized. They recall their identity in Christ. They proclaim to all, visible and invisible, that Jesus is victor over sin, death, and the devil.

I once felt so severely slandered by a demonic whisper while driving to work—a word that made me question my usefulness as a pastor—that I pulled my car over to the side of the road and spoke very clearly, "Devil, you can't have me. I am a baptized child of God. I belong to Jesus Christ." The dark demonic shadow that had overcome my spirit subsided quickly. The age-old question with which every individual wrestles—"Who am I?"—is answered by and in Jesus. What he thinks of you matters more than your own opinion of yourself. You are *his*—"I am the good shepherd. I know my own and my own know me" (John 10:14). This outstanding fact is an unshakeable assurance to pastors when they mistakenly believe that their ministry and personal identity is about them. It never is—it's always about Jesus!

Your Sins Don't Belong to You

Jesus took away your sins when he died on the cross. His bloody and agonizing crucifixion reveals what our sins did to him. Because "without the shedding of blood there is no forgiveness of sins" (Heb 9:22). Because "he made him to be sin who knew no sin, so that in him we might become the righteousness of God" (2 Cor 5:21), you can rejoice that your sins are carried by him. After all, if they are stuck to him, then you are free. The One on the cross invites into himself the bite of every imaginable fiery snake in our lives, so that we no longer need to suffer their poison.

I recall counseling a dismayed army sergeant who agonized over feelings of deep personal guilt. He was the only survivor of the team that he had led during a gunfight many years ago. He blamed himself for the losses. Finally, I said, "Brother, your garbage belongs to Christ. He paid a high price for it. He actually became the dumpster for your sins on Good Friday. So, for goodness' sake, stop stealing from him." He looked at me in shock and horror. Then, after a moment's reflection, he nodded and began to weep. He couldn't fathom anybody else wanting his burdens. We talked some more. Then we prayed together. His eyes brightened. He smiled. His conscience was cleansed (Heb 9:14). "If the Son sets you free, you will be free indeed" (John 8:36). He rejoiced in grace—momentarily.

The spiritual garbage from which he had been freed found a way to creep back into his heart—a phenomenon to which any honest pastor can relate, though we are pretty skilled at hiding it. With Adam as our forefather, original sin is common to all people, though its symptoms vary from person to person. The high moral qualification for the pastoral office means that the ways in which sin works in our lives can be subtle, but sin is still there. Thankfully, because of the redemptive work of the second Adam, Jesus Christ, the same gospel forgives us all of our sins. He has reconciled all things to himself "whether on earth or in heaven, making peace by the blood of his cross" (Col 1:20).

This young man's guilt returned—as it often does, when we doubt that we have been forgiven. Like Peter walking on water, the moment he doubted his Savior and turned his eyes from Jesus and back onto himself, he began to sink into the sea. Since we can't easily forget our old sins, the devil gets us to doubt that they are long forgiven. We all need a reminder from time to time.

After all, everything in pastoral ministry relates back to restoring sinful people to our holy God. Strangely, it is both the easiest and most difficult task because it presumes a radical belief: that

Christ's forgiveness is the solution to all the world's dilemmas. It is the only antidote to the sickness of sin. Though it is vaster than the sky above and closer to us than the air we breathe, it's of little advantage to anyone when unrecognized or disregarded. But each and every time the forgiveness of sins is pronounced, the devil's kingdom is rattled to its hellish core. All the angels in heaven rejoice over every repentance (Luke 15:10). The worst demonic attacks do not manifest themselves in haunted houses or poltergeists, but the devilish damage done through the guilt of sin. Pastors have the Christ-given power to lock the devil's lying voice away from the ears of their people and to unstop their ears so they can hear the sounds of heaven. That is why God has given the church the keys to his kingdom. Pastors should never lose sight of the esteemed task of administering them.

I do my best never to be personally horrified or surprised by the sins that are confessed to or shared with me, no matter how unusual or dark they happen to be. Whatever terrible thing someone confesses, I try my best with my tone, attitude, body language, and words to reinforce the notion that sin is the universal human condition. We are all equally condemned by the law of God, and though my sins are different, they aren't any lighter, at least in God's eyes.

I advise others to adopt the same practice in the ministry of deliverance. Even if you don't believe in their accounts of ghosts and the supernatural, when people claim to have been harassed by the paranormal, their feelings and fears are real. The solution is real as well. Even when evils are imagined or invented, or guilt can be attributed to distorted memories due to mental health issues or trauma, pastors still have a crucial role to play: we express the wonderful promise that "with his wounds we are healed" (Isa 53:5).

That army sergeant called me one quiet Saturday afternoon. He begged me to see him right away. I raced to his place, anticipating the worst. When I got there he said, "Can you tell me again that Jesus took away my guilt? I can't believe it." Couldn't this wait until Monday? Then I realized that he had his priorities in better order than me. I reminded him that God loved him. I pronounced to him once again that his sins—both old and new— are forgiven.

His concern was refreshing in a world that doesn't think of itself as sinful. His sadness chased him to Jesus, making it a hidden blessing.

Christians who aren't unsettled by their sins don't realize how amazing grace is.

Reconciliation with God: Not a One-Time Event

Whether one acknowledges it or not, "I believe; help my unbelief" (Mark 9:24) is the sincere confession of every humble Christian. Pastor and layperson alike, we all struggle with believing that God is as good as he says he is. Our faith naturally dwindles and necessitates spiritual refreshment. Sometimes we don't sense our weakness, and simply need to "have not seen and yet have believed" (John 20:29). At other times, we may still feel like a bag of bones nailed to a tree, even after lots of prayer and Bible reading, but the truth of the matter is, Jesus alone has been crucified. And if your sins are on him, they are no longer on you.

Whether it comes to offering care to those who are plagued by obvious shameful acts and believe the devil's lies that they have no hope, or those who experience subtle daily chipping at their Christian consciences by the demonic chisel of guilt, the solution remains the same. Whether the sins have been done to us or are ones we have committed, the poison is identical and so is the remedy.

Social workers say 70 percent of marriage counseling revolves around issues that require forgiveness. Psychologists categorize anger as a secondary emotion. It is a response to feelings of guilt, injustice, and fear.

Not only does Jesus pointedly address guilt with forgiveness, he also answers justice with grace and fear with love. We have all sinned in the courtroom of heaven. We should rightly fear God's wrath and judgment. And yet our good Lord has taken our place in that convicted criminal's chair, declaring us not guilty. We "are justified by his grace as a gift, through the redemption that is in Christ Jesus, whom God put forward as a propitiation by his blood, to be received by faith" (Rom 3:24–25). The Christian doctrine of justification by grace through faith is another way of saying that we believe that God has forgiven us all of our sins because of Jesus.

Reconciled with God, we are freed from all guilt and fear (Rom 6:22). We also reconcile with others, enabled by God "who through Christ reconciled us to himself and gave us the ministry of reconciliation; that is, in Christ God was reconciling the world to himself, not counting their trespasses against them" (2 Cor 5:18–19).

Pastors exemplify this process as "ambassadors for Christ" (2 Cor 5:20). A vital way we do this is through truth-telling, especially regarding guilt.

I know of one pastor who was so tired of a parishioner choosing not to confess his burden because he felt unworthy to receive freedom, that the pastor put his hand on his head and absolved him with some of the most precious language of his church tradition: "In and by the stead and command of my Lord Jesus, I forgive you all your sins." These kinds of daring pastoral interventions are emergencies. The angels do this often for us, even though we are not even aware of their intervening work. Similarly, God doesn't ask our permission to love us. And neither do his ordained and called pastors when it comes to their sheep.

CHAPTER 8

The Forgiveness of Sins

O Lamb of God, that takest away the sin of the
world, have mercy upon us.
—*The Litany*

SOME PEOPLE THINK IT'S OLD NEWS. OTHERS
take the gospel message for granted or treat God's
forgiveness as only applicable in the case of big
moral blunders. But if the cross of Christ is the
heart of the Christian faith, then the forgiveness
of sins is its pulse, beating unceasingly through the
body of Christ. Its rhythm resounds in Christians'
lives when they hear and speak words of reconciliation. If spiritual warfare could be reduced to
one word, it would be "forgiveness."

True Christian spirituality grows in no other
place than at the foot of the cross of Christ.[24]

Spiritual war can only succeed when Christians empty themselves of themselves, realizing that they have nothing to offer of their own accord. Unless we admit that we are helpless sinners, we are sure to fail in our fight against our enemies. We are at our weakest when we sense ourselves strongest (2 Cor 12:9). The daily acknowledgment of our humble state is answered with a ceaseless gospel promise: "Your sins are forgiven." In these words from our Lord, we have strength, hope, and help. Filled with his forgiveness and humbly hidden within his mighty and gracious armor, we confess victoriously: "The LORD is my strength and my shield; in him my heart trusts, and I am helped" (Ps 28:7).

One of the most ancient prayers of the church is the Jesus Prayer: "Lord Jesus Christ, Son of God, have mercy on me, a sinner." When this is sincerely prayed, Christians associate themselves with the tax collector in the temple who went away blessed, as opposed to the self-righteous Pharisee who thought that true religion was about something other than God's grace.

Our new life in the Spirit begins and ends with crucifying ourselves with Christ daily (Gal

2:20). The more cognizant we are of the depth of our sins, the more conscious we are the depth of his forgiveness and the merciful character of God. "I must decrease so Christ can increase" (John 3:30). Refreshed with his forgiveness, driven by his love, we are able to love by forgiving others their sins.

Because we are united to Christ's heart in repentance and forgiveness, his blood pumps through our own hearts and souls, producing acts and deeds of unfaltering love. Acknowledging that forgiveness never gets old compels us to approach others in the same way God has approached us— the fruit of the Spirit follow: "love, joy, peace, patience, kindness, goodness, faithfulness, gentleness, self-control" (Gal 5:22–23). Realistic ministry goals and expectations result when they are rooted in a compassionate approach to others. The ministry isn't characterized by power but mercy.

We are bombarded by sin from within and without. In some cases, we are the ones who have been wronged; in others, we are the wrongdoers. As the early Christian service Compline puts it: "Some of my sin I know—the thoughts and words and deeds of which I am ashamed—but some is known only to You."[25] Usually sin and all its consequences are tangled up in one big mess. Regardless of who is to blame, these webs tie us to the evil one and distance us from heaven unless addressed with forgiveness.

Darkness and light do not coexist in the kingdom of God. Only one person can deliver us from the sinful maze in which we find ourselves entrapped: Jesus. Healing from sin's damage does require action on our part. We forgive as Christ has forgiven us. When it comes to cruel crimes like sexual abuse or murder, it's obviously harder than it sounds. When pastors emphasize the unconditional love of Christ for all people, many misunderstand. The criminal must still pay for his crime, according to temporal laws. While some confuse the forgiveness of sins with the overlooking of sins, others mistakenly think that forgiving deeply injurious sins includes forgetting that they ever happened. Caring for the wounded souls of hurting people necessitates that clergy clearly communicate these distinctions.

SIN EXPLAINABLE BUT NOT EXCUSABLE

Forgiveness never excuses sins. Most people, but especially those who have suffered terrible injustices, think that forgiveness suggests the crime or sin wasn't a big deal. To the contrary, because so serious, the only way of effectively dealing with it is letting God handle it. Even when the laws of the land severely punish criminals for their crimes, it can never fix the damage caused or completely balance the scales of justice. The hurts remain. Resentment is inevitable. Only the forgiveness of sins can release sins from their source so that they can cling to Christ instead. And if they hang upon him, you are free from their grip.

Forgiveness regards every sin as substantial. None are insignificant or frivolous. Because each one is too heavy for us to carry, Jesus does it. That is why he came to earth, not "to judge the world but to save the world" (John 12:47).

"I forgive you." It may seem like an easy solution to a complex equation—just a few words, thoughts, and prayers. Yet it can be the most difficult thing in the world to say and mean. "Which is easier, to say, 'Your sins are forgiven,' or to say, 'Rise and walk'?" (Matt 9:5). Jesus' prayer, "Father, forgive them, for they know not what they do" (Luke 23:34), was closely followed by his agonizing cry, "My God, my God, why have you forsaken me?" (Matt 27:46). Though it wasn't easy, Christ forgave us out of love.

And his forgiveness empowers us to do likewise, just as he enabled Stephen, in the midst of being stoned to death, to cry out, "Lord, do not hold this sin against them" (Acts 7:60). It's not easy to desire, receive, or offer forgiveness, but "what is impossible with man is possible with God" (Luke 18:27).

Pastors must never cheapen grace, trivialize the severity of sin, downplay people's guilt—whether real or imagined—nor minimize the painful consequences of lingering sin. A shepherd's crook is used not only to catch and save sheep as they run away but also to keep them within the fold. When it comes to unforgiving attitudes, pastors have the difficult task of discerning when to use the holy Scriptures gently or severely. But in both cases, pastors always address their sheep directly with the words of Christ.

Sin Forgiven but Not Necessarily Forgotten

Some sin obviously can never be forgotten. Some sins are serious crimes and are addressed by the state accordingly. These have more profound mental and spiritual effects on those who do or suffer from them. A sexually abused individual will never forget those traumatic events.

Thankfully, even though you may not forget sins you have experienced, you can still move forward with forgiveness. Several years ago a news reporter told of a mother who lost her teenage son to a murder in a high school. A psychologically unstable student opened fire in a classroom. With tears flooding down her cheeks she told the murderer, on camera—a stone-faced young man who showed no remorse for his crime—that she forgave him and would pray for him.

The hurt would never go away. She would never forget that she had had a son! Fueled through God's grace, she was able to move on through forgiveness. Her faith manifested in love. Whether she meant to or not, she was even able to help the criminal find peace, since love always weakens the devil's grip on souls. "If your enemy is hungry, feed him; if he is thirsty, give him something to drink; for by so doing you will heap burning coals on his head" (Rom 12:20).

I often advise people having a hard time forgiving—especially when their offender won't admit or apologize—to behave as if they have forgotten, even if they haven't. Thinking and speaking in forgiving ways won't change the wrongdoer, but it will change you. Likewise, it's hard to pray for someone with whom you are angry. Forgiveness is normally a choice. When we want to forgive, we already have.

Because sin is a spiritual pollution that keeps us out of God's holy heaven, the pastor's main job is offering and facilitating the forgiveness of sins. As we've seen, a pastoral ministry is the "ministry of reconciliation" (2 Cor 5:18). Some church bodies label this pastoral authority and power, "the office of the keys." The releasing of people from the prison of their sins and the opening of the door to heaven is based on Jesus' own words, "If you forgive the sins of any, they are forgiven them" (John 20:23). Every pastor has different levels of skill being a troubleshooter, peacemaker, administrator, missionary, and so forth. Yet one thing that all these roles have in common, and which doesn't depend on the pastor's personal abilities or character traits, is delivering the forgiveness of sins. That is their primary responsibility. But it's not the only one.

Sometimes this pastoral responsibility includes the retention of forgiveness (John 20:23). By utilizing this unnerving tool the pastor is ultimately drawing attention to the liberating forgiveness that the member has inadvertently refused by willfully remaining in a state of unrepentance. Unfortunately, this power to excommunicate is often misunderstood. The church does not aspire to exclude sinners from fellowship. Instead, people who do not seek grace already stand condemned before God's holy throne (John 3:18). That said, pastors need to ensure that they aren't abusing their authority by using church discipline to punish those with whom they disagree. This exceptional tool must be handled with care. It is intended to lead those who have gone astray back to Jesus. Not all sheep will welcome this pastoral care. Jesus promises tragic yet unavoidable occasions when you will need to "shake off the dust from your feet" (Matt 10:14) and deliver someone over to Satan for a season, "that his spirit may be saved in the day of the Lord" (1 Cor 5:5). It's not easy being a father nor disciplining those you love (Heb 12:6).

It is easy to get distracted by this dual objective—forgiving (and, sometimes, retaining) sins—when many churches' chief mission seems to be thwarted by other ministry goals. Congregational vision statements driven by attempts to satisfy worldly concerns, no matter how well-intended, are a problem cross-denominationally. The work that Christ has mandated his church to do, the Great Commission (Mark 16:15), becomes derailed by sincere attempts to specialize in some particular aspect of Christian ministry. Certainly churches will exhibit external differences in customs, traditions, language, and so forth, but all should be pursuing this same calling. Just as God is one, so is his church. Forgiving sins isn't just a doctrinal statement to which you accede. Forgiving sins is the mission statement of the Lord's church.

Every church program should feed into and flow out of a congregational vision that cultivates an environment fostered by God's forgiveness in Christ, reflecting God's forgiveness in Christ, and offering God's forgiveness in Christ. It is the life-blood of his holy community. Christ's mission is "that he might create in himself one new man in place of the two, so making peace, and might reconcile us both to God in one body through the cross" (Eph 2:15–16). Forgiveness of sins indicates the reconciliation of sinful people with a holy and gracious God. Reflecting God's generosity has life-changing and societally transforming consequences. It is also critical to self-healing.

LACK OF FORGIVENESS DAMAGES SELF

When you don't forgive others—even when they don't apologize like you want—you are always worse off. The devil will replay the event in your head over and over like a broken record. We forget what the initial issue was and cling to a distorted version of the truth. The hurt, anger, and hatred can linger for years, even a lifetime. It tears us up inside. It transforms some into hardened, cynical souls.

What both good and bad angels know is that when we demand that our offender admit and confess before we will forgive, we remain the worst prisoners to their wrongs. Even for those who have suffered unspeakable crimes against their bodies—like in the tragic case of rape victims assaulted by strangers who they will never meet again—forgiveness is essential in order to release them from the personal prisons of shame, anger, and guilt into which they have been thrown. As Harold Senkbeil points out, "Guilt is sin committed; shame is sin suffered"—even when it's not your own![26] For whether it be sins we do or sins done against us, both can be all-consuming unless we address them with forgiveness. The blood of Jesus not only covers a multitude of sins but also the consequences of those sins (Jas

5:20). Jesus "heals the brokenhearted and binds up their wounds" (Ps 147:3). He cleanses souls and makes hearts pure even when we have been passive recipients of another person's hurtful or destructive actions. In some cases, pastoral care and counseling may take years. Though some scars will never fade, the gospel remains the healing medicine.

God is all about setting prisoners free (John 8:36), and he does it through what I call "blanket forgiveness." He covers all our spiritual filth with his grace—even our sin-tainted, half-hearted confessions. "Love covers a multitude of sins" (1 Pet 4:8). He even forgives us when we don't ask—our Father is more willing to forgive than we are to ask. He is committed to making sure nothing blocks our relationship with him. "'If we are faithless, he remains faithful—' for he cannot deny himself" (2 Tim 2:13).

Most people practice this kind of forgiveness throughout the day with those they know and love the most. Imagine a marriage which involved a daily inventory-taking of our spouse's sins against us and required each item to be acknowledged and forgiven before it was removed from the list. The marriage wouldn't survive. Yet we seem to set unrealistic expectations for our relationships with others—usually when we're looking for an excuse not to forgive. Even when sinfulness results in an argument with your spouse, you forgive one another without necessarily revisiting every detail of the disagreement.

After a rough day together, and so that the sun does not set on any angry hurtful or resentful feelings that we may be carrying around in our hearts, my family has a tradition of confessing our sins toward one another and receiving forgiveness from one another. Otherwise, we give the devil an easy opportunity to make matters worse. We make peace with God and one another by praying compline: "I confess to God Almighty, before the whole company of heaven and to you, my brothers and sisters, that I have sinned in thought, word and deed by my fault, by my own fault, by my own most grievous fault; wherefore I pray God Almighty to have mercy on me, forgive me all my sins, and bring me to everlasting life. Amen." Many of the specific sins of the day remain unspoken, but that doesn't mean there isn't remorse, repentance, and forgiveness. Praying together reminds us of this.

For Christians, all sins need to eventually be considered as water under the bridge of the cross and drowned in the baptismal flood of Christ's life-giving blood. No sin is greater than those we commit against God, and he refuses to keep a record of wrongs. Neither does he insist upon a comprehensive confession from the sincerely repentant. Unlike us sinners, who often only *tolerate* reconciliation with our neighbors, God looks forward to it.

Conditions for Reconciliation

Processes of reconciliation are not about giving but about receiving. On the one hand, some Christians beat themselves up over their sins, even though they have heard the good news. But God doesn't derive enjoyment from the confession of our sins; he enjoys taking our sins away. He eagerly awaits the chance to absolve us and restore us to a precious father-child relationship.

On the other hand, some Christians avoid taking responsibility for their sins. They rob God of the opportunity to make things right. This is especially true when we approach our sin insincerely and thus self-righteously, such as when we try to pin more fault on the offender than on ourselves. We want others to look worse than us. Like an accountant, we bring out the scales: for which part does our offender need to apologize, and for which part do I? We behave like children: "Johnny, say sorry for pulling your sister's hair, and Sally, *you* say sorry for calling your brother a jerk." It becomes a question of who goes first with "I forgive you, *but* ..." Yet unless forgiveness is sought, not just tolerated, it bears little fruit. Forgiveness is our chief opportunity to love. We betray ourselves as servants of another master when we behave as though forgiveness were conditional. Even after saying the right words and doing the right things, we still despise a fellow child of God.

When the demands we place upon others in reconciliation are based in cries for justice without grace, they become indecent and spiritually dangerous. We have all become too accustomed to this juvenile behavior in families and courts. Sadly, this same legalistic understanding of absolution can be found in the church. By contrast, Jesus loves his enemies, and that is why he forgives them. When we don't confess our unwillingness or inability to forgive others, we deprive God of the opportunity to show his love to us. After all, "where sin increased, grace abounded all the more" (Rom 5:20).

The Holy Spirit makes every kind of forgiveness possible. He heals even the most brutal wounds. For

Christians, forgiveness isn't optional. Just as absolution characterizes our Lord, it should characterize pastors. We aim to make it our lifestyle. Mercy treasures the smallest semblance of an apology or the tiny traces of changed behavior. We pastors are used to witnessing family feuds and dysfunctional relationships. We are accustomed to prayerfully trying to lead our people away from paths of revenge and self-pity to ones hedged with angels. Forgiveness is the key, but it comes in many shapes and colors. Pastoral ministry involves the application of law and gospel to hearts and lives that aren't identical.

We'll have days, like Moses, when we cry out: "Why did you give me these people?" Yet when the pastor realizes that his members may be asking God the same question about him, then he really understands what it means to be family. We learn to love each other to a greater degree than before, with the same love that Christ has for us. We walk together down the path of forgiveness while surrounded by rejoicing angels.

Pastors Also Need to Be Forgiven

Pastors need pastors. We need to confide in someone in whom we can trust. Whether it be from an ecclesiastical superior or a clergy friend, we need to hear that *our* sins are forgiven. Although we can read that in the Bible, other Christians offer us a gift when they echo it back to us. The incarnate Lord deigns to continue to act in incarnate ways—through other people.

Pastors need to hear that word of forgiveness often, because we mess up a lot. We laity and clergy alike all have our personal demons with whom we wrestle daily, but the serpents that prey upon the pastoral office seem particularly crafty. To complicate matters, as sinners, we all carry personal baggage into our calling. Some of us may have felt drawn to the ministry because we had unresolved spiritual struggles of our own. These things can get in our way when we are trying to share the gospel. Or we can become so preoccupied with our own downfalls that we neglect our responsibilities to others. The sins that we have done and the sins that have been done to us need to be addressed head-on.

INDIVIDUAL CONFESSION

The good news is that we possess the mighty weapons to confront the sins hidden in the most hard-to-reach corners of our lives. Telling your sins privately and individually to another Christian—or private confession with a skilled pastor or spiritual advisor—offers invaluable help. When he is courageous and bold enough to ask the tough questions and lead you to identify these dark areas of your life, then the Holy Spirit is actively at work exposing all of our "fruitless deeds of darkness" (Eph 5:11 NIV) so that "everything that is illuminated becomes a light" (Eph 5:13 NIV). Every idolized aspiration, misplaced love, or deranged thought is addressed with the grace of God. When you actively put yourself under an over-shepherd's scrutiny and regularly expose that which you would rather keep concealed, you are actually engaging in spiritual warfare. When you confess your sins, "resist the devil, and he will flee from you" (Jas 4:7).

Even if we believe that we do not have much to confess, God has much to say and give. After all, the gospel is God's word, not our own. It's the most powerful weapon of the spirit. It is also mighty means of polishing up your pastoral armor. Demons hate the simple gospel truth, "Your sins are forgiven" (Matt 9:5). And because they are stalking you as a pastor, seeking to dismantle your ministry and devour your flock, you cannot minister effectively with any unforgiven sin lingering in your heart or conscience. They are masters at convincing us that we are unfit and ill-equipped to minister in God's kingdom. Only after pastors receive God's forgiveness themselves can they effectively share it with others. An exterminator is of limited use if his own gear is infested with pests. God has given pastors the tools to care for souls, and it does take deliberate effort to make sure that they are in good working order.

One of my favorite churches is the Notre Dame Basilica in Montreal, Canada. The interior is richly decorated with Old Testament stories that point worshipers to the coming Messiah. A series of confessional boxes hug the sides of the long nave. At first you don't notice them, but once you do, you can't ignore them, for they are an essential component to another journey. The sanctuary is designed as a microcosm of our Christian walk from birth to death. Whenever a visitor walks in, they first pass the baptismal font, reminding them of their new birth in Christ. Then their eyes are directed from one confessional box to the next, each one reminding them of the need for daily repentance and forgiveness. Like steps up a staircase, they lead the Christian pilgrim up the center aisle to the principal piece of furniture, an altar, where the

sacrifice of God is consumed. The voyage culminates with feasting at the Lord's table, a reminder
of the eschatological feast to come. But you can't
skip to the glorious end without walking each brick
of the path.

Pastors can only walk with their members on
their journey in a convincing way if they set the
example themselves. Sometimes we don't start with
simple solutions to complex problems because we
lack faith in the message that we proclaim to others.
But the first solutions *are* simple: Talking to God
in prayer. Pastors visiting pastors. My best sermons are those preached to myself first. Whenever
I get choked up writing a sermon, I know that it
will strike other hearts just as hard as it has my
own. In those moments, I am less inclined to talk
at people and more inclined to listen to the word
of God *with* them. And I am a more empathetic
listener when I have shared my problems with
another. I am a more compassionate pastor when
I have confessed my sins to others. When I haven't
actively sought opportunities for confession, God
has done it for me.

We lay out our trash, hurt feelings, evils, and
so forth at the garbage pit of Calvary. In confession, your Heavenly Father tells you, as if you are

the only person alive, "I love you." No Christian believer—young, old, pastor, or layperson—can hear that too often.

GOD EVEN USES EVIL FOR GOOD

Confessing one's sins can even become a cheerful opportunity to meet with God. The devil throws our sins at us, and God turns them into something worthwhile, inciting spiritual growth and deepening our faith. He turns "a parched land into springs of water" (Ps 107:35). Every Satanic assault has a boomerang effect when we repent. As was the case on Golgotha, God uses the worst tragedy imaginable to achieve his most benevolent purpose: to save humankind. "All things work together for good, for those who are called according to his purpose" (Rom 8:28). God's kind and gracious character is unconceivably good.

Attacks in the ministry—suffering and sorrows—are inevitable. Yet they are not only to be tolerated but even welcomed and embraced. For God uses Satan to keep us humble and to chase us to the cross. Like Job, who was totally unaware of the conversation between God and the devil, we don't get access to God's hidden will—and this is precisely why the story of Job remains such an encouragement to us. We, too, don't usually understand the reasons for our suffering. When we feel like the devil has taken control of our lives, when not even our friends are a reliable source of support, nor reason a way of understanding, we may remain confident that God has permitted the evil for the sake the ultimate good. When the devil's schemes drive us back to seek God's mercy, we see clearly how he serves as a divine instrument, leading us to cling more tightly to Jesus Christ.

Even the devil remains a servant of God, whether he likes it or not. God's love for us is so great that he even uses the demons for our good, to the devil's eternal frustration. We encounter this best in Jesus, the ultimate example of this truth. All Christians are "becoming like him in his death" (Phil 3:10), so our own suffering should never surprise us. Even when we feel ourselves defeated by the devil, we have great hope, when we allow those evils to bring us back to our Savior, Lord, and friend, Jesus Christ. In his cross and resurrection, we remain victorious, despite our feelings or experiences.

Just as awareness of good angels should drive us to our knees in worship, the realization that bad angels are hard at work should drive us to our knees in prayer. Spiritual warfare is real and requires each Christian to take up arms. Yet instead of turning inside to ourselves for help, we flee to God for mercy.

Consider the disciples in Mark 17, who are mystified by their inability to cast out certain demons. Some biblical manuscripts cite Jesus informing the disappointed disciples that those demons could only be exorcized by "fasting and prayer" (Matt 17:21). Many take this to mean that if the disciples had only fasted to strengthen themselves, they would have been successful. But I wonder if the real issue was that the disciples were growing too confident in themselves. The most unnatural thing in the world is to deny oneself, and yet it is precisely in those moments that we take a leap of faith. We jump away from ourselves and hold instead to Christ. There, we receive the support that only our Lord can give. And the most prominent time and place to receive that care is in worship.

CHAPTER 9

The Victory of Worship

*Let my prayer rise before You as incense and the
lifting up of my hands as the evening sacrifice.*
—Psalm 141:2, Psalmody for Evening Prayer

PASTORS ARE STEWARDS OF THE MYSTERIES OF
God (1 Cor 4:1). We are like the butlers of the
Lord's estate. We care about how our master's
guests are treated and how they act in his royal
house. But sometimes we get sloppy. We forget
who we are and where we are. We get fooled
into believing that we are organizational leaders,
community coordinators, or theological educators. Because of our natural inclination to trust
our eyes—and it doesn't look like anything really
special is happening in church—we act as if we
aren't in the holy presence of God. Yet what we

see isn't what we get. We see only regular people, simple bread, boring water, and often empty pews. But what we get is saints of heaven, the body of Christ, living water, and a church filled with angels.

Going to Church Matters

Public worship is essential in spiritual warfare. Insisting that Christians go to church isn't legalistic. Church is an opportunity to meet with God as the incarnate Word of God from heaven enters into our human space. We are the envy of the angels because God became human and dwelt among us.[27]

By making these dwelling places his temporary home, the church buildings where we meet are likened to embassies of heaven. We are in God's home every time two or three gather in the name of the Father, Son, and Holy Spirit (Matt 18:20). To remind us of this fact, some churches design the altar at the front of the sanctuary to look like a little castle that has dropped from heaven to earth. Heaven comes to earth as our Lord manifests himself among us in Christian worship.

The privilege of intimately meeting with God wasn't easily secured. Consider the warnings, rules, and regulations in the Old Testament restricting people from approaching God's holiness. Animals were endangered by their very proximity to the foothills of Mount Sinai. Even the reflection of the backside of God's glory on Moses's shining face was almost too much for people to bear (Exod 34:35), so he had to wear a veil. Yet because of Jesus' death and resurrection, we have been granted safe access to God's glory. Christ is our ark of the covenant. Though he is our friend, we must still be cautious. We are not equals. Our Lord "is the same yesterday and today and forever" (Heb 13:8), and our ability to approach our holy God doesn't mean we can approach worship casually. Our glorious and majestic Lord is present today in an even greater way than he was in the Old Testament. Like the priests of the Old Testament, we must handle with care the sacred practices that our Lord has passed on to us through his church (2 Thess 2:15).

Even when the early Christians gathered to worship in catacombs, they did their best to organize their spaces to look like synagogues, which resembled the Jerusalem temple. After all, Christian worship wasn't considered to be a new kind of worship but rather a fulfillment of Old

Testament forms. The Levitical priests would never have dreamed that the coming of Immanuel meant that their successors would have such easy access to the God who resided within the holy of holies. A more wonderful and magnificent holy conversation than theirs happens in church services than was ever imagineable in Temple worship. We encounter God directly through Christ, "for God, who said, 'Let light shine out of darkness,' has shone in our hearts to give the light of the knowledge of the glory of God in the face of Jesus Christ" (2 Cor 4:6).

God Works on Sundays

"The Son of Man came not to be served but to serve" (Matt 20:28). He loves us so much that he visits us in person Sunday after Sunday. In these special moments, we are likened to Mary—we receive gifts of heaven more valuable than all the treasures in the world, purchased and won for us, not with gold or silver but with the innocent suffering and atoning death of Jesus. There is a time for us to serve, like Martha, but this is not it. There is one exception: pastors. Christ continues to serve his people in worship, and he does it through his called and ordained ministers.

Worship, then, is not primarily about us telling God how wonderful he is. Worship services are God's moment to work on us. He helps us recover from the wounds of a week's worth of spiritual war and lift us up again. Jesus' blood is the balm for all our battle wounds. His promises refresh us. The songs and hymns that we sing and the sermons that we hear are mainly for our sake, too. They remind each believer that "The LORD is the stronghold of my life—of whom shall I be afraid?" (Ps 27:1). It is fitting that God does most of the talking, and he chooses to do it through the mouth of his shepherds.

God's creatures are hardwired to be in a worshipful relationship with their Creator. Pastors keep them connected with their Lord not only through one-on-one caregiving but also by encouraging the congregation of Christian pilgrims on the road to glory. When pastors cultivate an atmosphere of worship that allows these future citizens of heaven to delight in their scheduled appointment in one of God's many embassies, the journey through life doesn't seem as monotonous. For "things into which angels long to look" (1 Pet 1:12) happen at these spiritual pit stops. When pastors show piety and reverence toward these mysteries of faith, they inspire the same attitude in those they lead.[28]

Worship as a Picture of Heaven

The book of Revelation offers the best window into what's happening in worship. It paints a picture of the dominance of the church triumphant over the kingdom of darkness, now and until the end of the world. St. John's vision was intended to strengthen and encourage persecuted Christians who thought that God had abandoned them (Rev 2:10). The faithful are prompted not to trust what they see with their eyes but to believe God's holy word.

Take Revelation 8:3, for example. We encounter angels and saints—our believing loved ones— with whose prayers our own are mingled: an angel "was given much incense to offer with the prayers of all the saints on the golden altar before the throne." Incense, in the Bible, evokes temple worship. As smoke ascended to heaven from the altar of incense in the tent of meeting, it mixed with the odor of the burnt sacrifice that atoned for the people's sins. Through this sacrifice—which prefigures Christ, the ultimate sacrifice—faithful followers were permitted to come into God's presence and offer their requests at the mercy seat of God. God almighty, hidden within the holy of holies, invisible behind a curtain and within a cloud, promised to hear their prayers. It was as if his own Son were making the plea as "the smoke of the incense, with the prayers of the saints, rose before God from the hand of the angel" (Rev 8:4).

One of my favorite evening prayers is "let my prayer be counted as incense before you" (Ps 141:2). It reminds me that my priestly intercessions for the world are intermingled with Christ's and those of the entire white-robed army of saints and martyrs in one common supplication. Just as a petition carries more weight when it contains many signatures, so too my pastoral prayers seem stronger when endorsed by these holy ones.

The vision given to John in Revelation was sent to comfort God's people by pronouncing, as we discussed in chapter 1, that *the* church is bigger than *your* church:

> Around the throne were twenty-four thrones, and seated on the thrones were twenty-four elders, clothed in white garments, with golden crowns on their heads. From the throne came flashes of lightning, and rumblings and peals of thunder, and before the throne were burning seven

torches of fire, which are the seven spirits of God, and before the throne there was as it were a sea of glass, like crystal. (Rev 4:4–6)

Because heaven is so otherworldly, the best way of describing these spiritual phenomena is through symbolic language. Even the numbers in this vision express deep theological significance. "Twenty-four elders" is a numerical expression of all the people of God from both Old Testament and New: the twelve tribes of Israel plus the twelve apostles. The population of heaven consists of all believers whose names are written in the Lamb's book of life (Rev 21:27). Even though they may still reside on earth, heaven is their home.

Worship as a Massive Family Reunion

Historically, the rail around some church altars was a semicircle, since the full circle was completed on the other side of the wall—where the cemetery lay. This architectural layout expresses the union between worshipers on earth and in heaven when we gather for worship at church. Whether it be the cancer patient who painfully passed before our eyes in the palliative care unit, the young man tragically killed in a car wreck and survived by his grieving wife, or the stillborn baby of a young, heartbroken couple, each and every lost loved one is closer to us than we think. As a pastor of a liturgical church, I have found that the words sung at the beginning of our Communion service, "with angels and archangels and all the company of heaven, we laud and magnify your glorious name," often bring deep comfort to my grieving parishioners. The faithfully departed belong to that "company of heaven." Even though we can't communicate with them, we will remain united for all eternity.

Worship is like a massive family reunion. We join with our deceased brothers and sisters in praying to, praising, and worshiping the eternal God. Just as they once did on earth, they continue to adore their Lord in heaven. They participate in the joyous events anticipating the eternal party scheduled at the end of time. "You have come to Mount Zion and to the city of the living God, the heavenly Jerusalem, and to innumerable angels in festal gathering" (Heb 12:22). No wonder the Bible compares heaven to a wedding feast.

In addition to being close to our believing loved ones, we are also in close proximity to the innumerable army of heavenly hosts who minister alongside us. Our heavy burdens and our grievances against God look tiny in the holy moment of worship. The hills that we thought we had to die on—whether they were true or imaginary—appear microscopic next to the triumphant tree of life upon which Jesus hung.

In this vision of the saints and angels worshiping together in an unending hymn, the music drowns out our individual egos. The enormous size of the celestial city puts our lifespans into perspective. We cast our crowns—all that has been achieved in life through our words and deeds—at the foot of the Lamb's royal throne (Rev 4:10). Our work is done, and we are forever protected from harm and danger. "Then I looked, and I heard around the throne and the living creatures and the elders the voice of many angels, numbering myriads of myriads and thousands of thousands, saying with a loud voice, 'Worthy is the Lamb who was slain, to receive power and wealth and wisdom and might and honor and glory and blessing!' And I heard every creature in heaven and on earth and under the earth and in the sea, and all that is in them, saying, 'To him who sits on the throne and to the Lamb be blessing and honor and glory and might forever and ever!' " (Rev 5:11–13).

What an uplifting vision! All the hosts of heaven, pastors and people, saints and angels, unite in awe and celebration—singing, communing, joining in prayer, praising God, and saying, "Hosanna!"

In church we don't pretend that God is present. God is really with us! And the entire company of heaven is there too. Yet they remain hidden from our eyes; we hear and see nothing extraordinary. The music, lighting, images, and colors—and, in some churches, incense, priestly vestments, and paraments—are intended to help us feel that we have joined the festivities of heaven. Bright and colorful stained-glass windows in ancient cathedrals are meant to remind worshipers that they are surrounded by holy ones who pervade our sacred space with their shining light and glorious splendor. Yet even the most decorated churches cannot completely convey the wondrous ways in which heaven and earth are joined in collective worship. The angelic courtiers surround Jesus, humanity's ladder to heaven, upon whom the holy angels ascend and descend, caring for all of our needs. Whether our worship services are big or small, rich or poor, when we worship according to the holy word of God, our holy God is present.

REVERENCE AND PRAYER

When it comes to worship, a faithful pastor ought to do his best to actively establish a reverent atmosphere in the sanctuary, even when his church meets in a school gymnasium, a strip mall, or the outdoors.

Because angels worship the Lord unceasingly in heaven, they are present at the gateway to the heavenly realm—at times of prayer and in places of worship. If the angels fall on their faces in the presence of God, we likewise need to behave in ways befitting that sacred space. Just as the Levites carried the ark of the covenant with scrupulous and great care, pastors are appointed by God to practice their ministry with the highest degree of reverence. We Christians have gotten so used to the idea that Jesus is our friend that we sometimes forget that he is also almighty God and King of kings. But the angels never forget where they are. Church father Clement of Rome described it like this:

> Let us think of the whole host of angels, how they stand by and serve his will, for Scriptures say: "Ten thousand times ten thousand were doing service to him, and they cried out: Holy, holy, holy, Lord Sabaoth; the whole of creation is full of his

glory." Then let us gather together in awareness of our concord, as with one mouth we
shout earnestly to him that we may become
sharers in his great and glorious promises.[29]

Good things stand the test of time, and the
writings of our Christian forefathers have weight.
They are like giants upon whose shoulders we
stand. Ministry isn't about one single angel but
one common service for one common Lord. Our
pastoral ministry is best when it connects people
to a Jesus and his church that surpass one single
lifetime, that is rooted in history and the timeless
Scriptures.

As a chaplain I have given many soldiers
a copy of the evening compline[30] service that
they could fold it up in the back pocket of their
uniform and pray in whatever foxholes, literal
or metaphorical, they found themselves. One
tough infantryman who was a newly converted
Christian thanked me for his with tears in his
eyes. He said that he didn't know the Bible very
well, but he loved those Bible verses on that wrin-
kled-up sheet and was dedicated to reading the
prayers: "Be our light in the darkness, O Lord,
and in your great mercy defend us from all perils

and dangers of this night," or, "Visit our dwellings, O Lord, and drive from them all the snares of the enemy; let your holy angels dwell with us and preserve us in peace." Praying prewritten prayers can amount to letting someone else carry us in moments of tiredness and frailty.

Despite its brief length and simple words, the Lord's Prayer addresses the entire complex human condition. Ancient prayers stand the test of time. They resonate in Christian hearts with the same rigor today as they did thousands of years ago. There is also a lovely consolation and encouragement repeating the same words as my brothers and sisters in Christ have prayed in other times in history. They underwent the same kinds of challenges and made it to heaven. When prayed from the heart, such liturgies permit a continuity and uniformity with the larger Christian population—in both time and space—that edifies our souls in indescribable ways. This is what that soldier was getting at. He was part of something bigger and it didn't matter that he felt himself small.

So often churches feel that they need to give people a compelling reason to come to church. We lean on flashy programs, marketing techniques, or entertaining messages to try to compete with the most attractive churches in town. But the sweet gospel is appetizing in itself to those in whom God is at work. It doesn't require any frills or extra trimmings. The most compelling reason to come to church can be summarized in this simple invitation: "Do you want to meet with God? Do you want to see Jesus?" Whether the invitees respond positively or negatively is not your concern. We are only asked to plant the seeds, tell the truth, and ensure that we are faithful stewards of God's home and gifts. Leaving the rest up to God and his harvesters, we can all confess together with Simeon, having gazed upon the glory of the infant Savior: "Lord, now you are letting your servant depart in peace, according to your word; for my eyes have seen your salvation that you have prepared in the presence of all peoples, a light for revelation to the Gentiles, and for glory to your people Israel" (Luke 2:29–32). True worship always culminates in reverential prayer. When Scripture is spoken with faith, the voice of God is heard by everyone in attendance. Not only does it deliver to God's people what it promises, but it also silences the devil who remains speechless before the saints of God and his heavenly hosts. The spoken word of God always exorcizes demons.

Satan Keeping People from Worship

No wonder the devil is so determined to get people away from church, the place where our Lord continues to be present in very real ways. The benefits of the incarnation didn't stop the moment Jesus ascended into heaven. Jesus disappeared from the eyes of the disciples, as "a cloud took him out of their sight" (Acts 1:9), but that didn't mean that he was no longer bodily there with them. Otherwise they wouldn't have been encouraged by the angels' assurance, "Men of Galilee, why do you stand looking into heaven? This Jesus, who was taken up from you into heaven, will come in the same way as you saw him go into heaven" (Acts 1:11). Although a mystery, the fact that our God who "became flesh and dwelt among us" (John 1:14) is not a distant god is the greatest conceivable morale boost in spiritual war.

Some pastors seem resigned to their sheep's poor church attendance or infrequent use of God's sacred gifts. They have probably tolerated it as a survival technique after years of watching members sadly slip away from the faith. But whatever parishioners' stated reasons might be, infrequent visits to God's house are not excusable. Skipping church is not only damaging to ourselves, it is a great insult to God. (Imagine declining an invitation from the king or president to dine in their private quarters!) Pastors can't force their people to attend church more often, but they are remiss when they cease praying for and teaching a higher view of worship. In our rationalistic, secularist age, Christians need constant reminders that the heavenly treasures that are uniquely available in the church are as valuable as the Bible claims.

If people believed in what was actually happening in your church, there would be lines of people begging to enter. The angels don't need to be compelled. Unlike us sinners, they find their deepest sense of fulfilment in worshiping in the eternal church service, to which we have a portal and, thus, receive a delightful foretaste of the feast to come. Work schedules, sports tournaments, or social commitments are deplorable excuses for poor attendance stemming from lack of faith. When God is the host, we never have a good reason to decline his invitation to this festive banquet (Luke 14:12–24).

Worship serves as the long-awaited water station in a marathon that begins the instant that we become Christians. The all-too-familiar hecklers of the world, the devil, and the old self do their best to prevent us tired athletes from getting to water coolers conveniently positioned at regular seven-day intervals. After all, "the water that I will give him will become in him a spring of water welling up to eternal life" (John 4:14). On the one hand, one tiny drop from his vitalizing cup is sufficient. On the other hand, because of our self-inflicted fears and doubts, it's imperative that we come and drink over and over. Certainly, with Jesus as our living water (John 4:1–15), the devil cannot seriously harm us. But he can still do some memorable damage. All temptation to neglect public worship arises from devilishly designed tactics to keep Christians from gathering together in the unassailable places that God meets us with his divine presence. The best way of doing this is making us think that it's not essential to our spiritual health.

Yet it's not the building that matters. It's who meets us inside that counts. The Israelites grieved the rebuilding of the Second Temple because it was missing one important item: the ark of the covenant. God was with them through that holy object. And so too God meets us in his home "in spirit and truth" (John 4:24). Outside is darkness, because Jesus is "the light of the world" (John 8:12). Still, those who abstain from God's word and service are living in a hell on earth that continues in the afterlife. In the end, those who wanted God to leave them alone in life get what they requested— his absence.[31] Those who despised worship on earth aren't forced to tolerate it in heaven. God created people to find their resting place in him, and so those who reject him will remain unfulfilled. Just as Christians have a foretaste of heaven *inside* Christianity, so unbelievers have a foretaste of hell *outside* the one true faith.

Accordingly, some churches are in the shape of an ark or ship. Images of anchors are sometimes used. Christians enter the safety of God's boat through the waters of baptism (1 Pet 3:20–21), which carries them through the sinful seas of life. Those outside the ark deprive themselves of the Lord's saving Word. Christ's voice, heard through the lips of his ministers, is often the only thing keeping us afloat on the waves of trials, suffering, and temptation.

Demons are unable to sabotage the worship of heaven, but they can hassle us at these earthly portals, where our Lord's ambassadors serve his heavenly citizens. They also get into the individual temples of our souls, distracting us from God's word and causing us to question his promises.

Yet the Lord is committed to us. When we, like Thomas, question the reality of Jesus' presence, his word transforms our doubts into faith. This happens through and by pastors in worship. No wonder they are often so deeply attacked.

Satan Distracting Pastors in Worship

Both pastors and laypeople are tempted to believe that what is going on in worship is not special. But when we refuse to give in to this reasoning, and keep up the good fight in our preaching, teaching, and leading in worship, we torment demons. The intensity of spiritual war escalates in these particular times and places. Our fatigue cannot just be attributed to the pressures of public speaking or being in the public eye. The devil wants to tire you out. He is hard at work within congregations and ministries that are faithful to the gospel. The demons attack what they fear. Because true teaching and preaching are major components of worship services, they are petrified of services that highlight who God is and what he has done to save the world. They don't want us to hear that we are justified entirely by the Lord's grace through faith. They would rather we hear lists of tasks we must do to improve our spiritual walks. They tremble at the fact that Jesus' word becomes our word, which equips us for battle against them. Jesus confronts them through Christian voices, those of both pastors and believing people. The message of Christ—his words and atoning work at the cross—rightly terrifies and sends them running.

Testing the Spirits of Teaching

As pastors, we are not immune from shifting our focus away from Christ. And so, we ought to examine ourselves daily: "Beloved, do not believe every spirit, but test the spirits to see whether they are from God, for many false prophets have gone out into the world" (1 John 4:1). Testing the spirits doesn't only involve assessing the teachings of others but also evaluatvaing ourselves as shepherds, making sure that our teaching fully aligns with the Bible. "Keep a close watch on yourself and on the teaching. Persist in this, for by so doing you will save both yourself and your hearers" (1 Tim 4:16). When Zechariah doubts the angel Gabriel's word regarding his barren wife Elizabeth's pregnancy—demanding some proof that God can achieve this miracle—he loses his speech (Luke 1:5–23). Although it's a divine punishment, it's also a safety net to both the proclaimer and his hearers. The pure and precise word is so precious that God ensures that this preacher gets some mandatory time off. After a time of repentance, he is filled with a new humility and faith and is even better at his pastoral tasks of proclaiming and praising God.

Neglecting to examine ourselves and our doctrine can lead to clumsy decisions. Some clergy may find themselves under immense pressure to change worship styles because their people have gotten bored. Although traditions are not set in stone, Christians are wise to respect those who have traveled the journey before us. Wisdom comes with age. Our ancient Christian brothers and sisters shared many of our same struggles and temptations.

The cross of Christ is never attractive to the old Adam in us. We glory in it anyway, since it remains the only certain and timeless truth in our world. "But far be it from me to boast except in the cross of our Lord Jesus Christ, by which the world has been crucified to me, and I to the world" (Gal 6:14). Accordingly, the church's theological principles arising from the Holy Bible must be the determining factor in pastoral decisions. We are careful not to cater to our "own passions" (2 Tim 4:3) and preferences, "teaching as doctrines the commandments of men" (Matt 15:9).

But though pastors lead the church, it doesn't belong to them alone. We steward God's house and its people with great care. When the prefect of Rome asked St. Lawrence to bring out all the treasures of the church so he could steal them, this Christian brother brought out the poor. Yet because "the work of God" isn't about works but faith—"that you believe in him whom he has sent" (John 6:29)—the best tool that clergy can offer people is helping them believe rightly and developing a good theological filter through which to process the information constantly bombarding them. We can assist our parishioners in generating a sense of theological smell to discern truth from error. The church has always answered the question, "How do we test the spirits?" by, at the very least, filtering contemporary theology, politics, and culture through the Ten Commandments, the Apostles' Creed, and the Lord's Prayer. Limiting our Bible studies to moralistic, trite lessons does not equip the saints in this present age. Mature, deliberate Christian education and catechesis is necessary to keep them safe and ready for warfare. Even if they can't precisely discern the origin of the fire, they can still smell the smoke.

Pastors need to be careful not to teach over people's heads. At the same time, assuming that our people are incapable of doing theology is an equally dangerous pitfall as they encounter unchristian opinions throughout the week at work, home, and school. Because every Christian has the responsibility to "work out your own salvation with fear and trembling" (Phil 2:12), pastors equip their sheep for spiritual warfare by helping them discern between the spirits of diverse doctrines. They may hear solid teaching in the sermon. But there are many other voices that compete with Christ's throughout the week, when you are not there. Keeping in touch, building relationships, and encouraging Bible studies keeps them grounded in the word between Sundays. Clearly, articulating the truth is best done when you identify and debunk these lies masquerading as truth. Our people are bombarded daily with worldly opinions. Good teaching on Sundays provides armor for the week's warfare—at work, home, and school—where most of our battles are fought. And, in Christ, all of these battles are won.

CHURCH ISN'T JUST ON SUNDAYS

Angels are not only present at Sunday worship—their angelic ministry continues throughout the week. And as discussed in chapter 2, pastors are angels to their people. The language and heavenly sound that echoes through our souls from public church services reverberates into our daily prayer life, family devotions, and worship at home. This is why scheduled worship throughout the week, or even every day, is beneficial. In the midst of the fatiguing spiritual war in which Christians are attacked relentlessly by sin, the world, and the devil, time spent with God in church and Bible reading is our resting place.

As a chaplain, when people would apologize to me for interrupting me with their crises and problems, I would say, "To the contrary, I thank you for offering me another occasion to take some time in prayer." The toils of others are actually a gift to you. They avail you of the chance to polish your spiritual armor and put it to good use.

In addition to personal prayer, orders of service can be used at home, with huge benefits for our spiritual health. The COVID-19 stay-at-home order in Canada allowed my family to have more elaborate devotion times than we had been able to have in our pre-pandemic life. When the Reformers closed the monasteries in medieval Germany, their hope was that the best parts of monastic life would continue in the home. This included daily morning prayer and evening worship services. The parents, as the heads of the household, acted as abbots, educating children, praying for both church and state, and leading communal adoration of our holy Triune God. Such familial piety seasons our conversations with friends and our family discussions at the dinner table.

The pastor helps to cultivate this piety too. He doesn't stop shepherding when he exits the building. Instead, he guides his flock with a keen eye for how to help them import worship into their own households. These too can become small fortresses in the church's defense against the enemy. Some churches end their services with a recessional in which a cross is paraded out of the sanctuary and into the narthex. The cross of Christ is being carried into the world. Sunday worship continues, throughout the week, in various forms and ways. It's normal and natural for pastors to find themselves offering the same blessings of corporate Sunday worship in more private venues. What follows are some specific facets of ministry and worship outside corporate Sunday worship services.

Homes as Houses of Worship

House blessings are a good way to help people realize that their homes are mini-churches or chapels, spaces dedicated to the Lord's use. At the very least, they give the pastor a chance to offer advice on worship and prayer life at home, even to commend people for Bible-verse magnets on their fridges or crosses on their walls, or address any suspicious occult or other unbefitting objects. Beginning with a Trinitarian invocation, the pastor processes with the family from room to room, praying, even dedicating, the space to the Lord's service. Scriptures are read in each room that pertain to the various dimensions of Christian family life. The kitchen is not simply a place to cook, but a chance to remember our spiritual nourishment and offer thanks to God for our daily bread. The spare bedroom becomes an appeal to show hospitality to strangers and a means by which Christians are to share the friendship of God. The office is described in ways that assume the study of God's holy word as the source of all wisdom and guidance for those dwelling under the roof of this holy house. The pastor addresses the family with a message, as he would the congregation with a sermon. A creed is confessed together, the Our Father prayed, a couple of hymns sung, and a blessing given—the event resembles a Sunday worship service in many respects.

The true objective is to help the faith community appreciate their daily routine as an extension of church worship. Appreciating the sacredness of the space in which we dwell has practical implications as well. If kind language, edifying media, and holy ways are appropriate in church, then why not at home too? Viewing my home as a spiritual temple leads to viewing my heart as one, too. Some Christians pray a liturgical rite, intended for public worship, at home: "For *this holy house* and for all who offer *here* their worship and praise, let us pray to the Lord."[32] Congregational worship is a special moment with God and critical to our spiritual health and safety, yet worship also extends beyond Sunday morning.

Shut-In Visits

Many pastors offer home communion visits for the sick, shut-ins, or elderly to help maintain the bridge between the homebound member and the wider body of Christ. Some pastors take conse-crated bread from the preceding Sunday worship service instead of repeating a separate service, lest the visit begin to resemble a separate church. It's also a demonstration of the continuity between the individual and the larger church. The isolated Christian still gets to participate in the same wor-ship service. Though consumed on different days, the church remains one loaf, one bread. We build up the unified, single body of Christ when we join God's people together. In these home visits, we cast out Satan from the hearts of members confined to their homes, members who may feel abandoned because they aren't able to join others in fellowship. By helping parishioners see that they aren't battling their demons alone but are part of the larger body, we better maintain a united stronghold.

Emergency House Calls

Some home visits may require different tools—ones you don't often have cause to use—to chase away the devil. As in New Testament times, Jesus remains the exorcist, and he casts out demons through his word.

The practice of the ministry of deliverance can be summarized as the prayerful verbalization of biblical phraseology. When ministering to those who are demonically oppressed, pastors employ the same phrases used in church. They often begin "in the name of the Father, Son, and Holy Spirit," reminding everyone present that, no matter how tormented the soul is or how ugly the body appears, it belongs to God. During an exorcism, they speak the same Scriptures that are heard in church. After all, prayers like the Lord's Prayer or the Christian creeds are as distasteful to the devil outside church buildings as within.

The intent of speaking Bible verses and Christian prayers aloud is to make it so uncomfortable for the evil entities that they flee. Demons hate hearing about Jesus. Remember the "rat principle"? You get a rat out of a house in two ways: poisoning it, or removing its food source. When pastors repeat the vocabulary of worship with Bible verses, rebukes, and prayers, they poison these spiritual rats.

Demons want to minimize the vocalization of these gospel declarations and may increase their disruptive efforts. Regardless of how diabolical entities rant and rave, pastors need to be firm and unwavering in faith. Most of all, pastors need to believe that they have been called to bring God's presence to these people and places. But be fore-warned, once the demon departs, the minister's work has just begun. He must make sure recovering Christians keep their houses tidy from spiritual uncleanliness—not only in the relatively simple steps of getting rid of occult objects and so forth but also in adopting a routine of prayer, Bible study, church celebrations, and sacramental services. Pastors who parachute into people's lives, caring for them only in moments of crisis, aren't as effective servants as those shepherds who abide near their lambs throughout their lives. Some of those lambs may require more attention than others—some lambs may still be goats! But you didn't land in their lives by accident. God brought you to them.

Fostering Personal Relationships

The healthiest shepherding relationships happen in one-on-one settings. When the ratio between pastor and people is too great, how can the pastor really be involved in the lives of his members as a spiritual guide?

Having moved around a lot for work when I served as a military chaplain, I have often chosen small congregations as my family's worshiping community. With five children, finding a scriptural

When we are found near our people in the mud and filth, we also find Jesus. He is there serving and saving them.

FOLLOW THE LEADER

Pastors set the example. When pastors carefully handle and highly value their pastoral office and divine call, so will those they lead. But if pastors don't wholeheartedly believe they are God's instruments, serving in God's holy place, neither will their flock appreciate the profound gifts that they receive.

Even when pastors buy into the lie that what's happening in church isn't exceptional, that Christians are merely reacting to conceptualizations of a distant God rather than enjoying real interactions with an intimately present Lord, others are still enraptured. Remember this: angels and demons are roused and provoked in public worship. And by virtue of your alliance with the angels and allegiance to the Lord, an agitated devil, who considers you a terrifying threat, must ultimately admit that you and your people are beyond his grasp.

CHAPTER 10

Priests Equipping Priests

Keep us firm in the true faith throughout our days of
pilgrimage that, on the day of His coming, we may,
together with all Your saints, celebrate the marriage
feast of the Lamb in His kingdom which has no end.
—Post-Communion Collect

GOD DISTRIBUTES HIS SPIRITUAL WEAPONS
and wisdom to his people through his pastors.
This dynamic is a primary benefit of public worship. As John Bunyan so judiciously described the
Christian journey, we are earthly pilgrims with
eyes fixed on our eternal resting place. And we
are not alone. A gracious flow of celestial energy
from our heavenly home is poured into the earthly
embassies of local Christian congregations enliven-
ing us in our spiritual soldiering: "And we all, with

unveiled face, beholding the glory of the Lord, are being transformed into the same image from one degree of glory to another. For this comes from the Lord who is the Spirit" (2 Cor 3:18).

The word, message, gifts, and even glory are received by faith by God's royal priests (1 Pet 2:9) who then transmit them to the world around them in their sanctified thoughts, words, deeds, witness, and a bold public confession of their faith. The gospel is contagious, and new soldiers are born. Like a ray of light that, after striking a diamond, is refracted into a multiplicity of other magnificent beams, the grace that we have received in the worship service is reflected in all the wondrous works of God's Spirit in Christian lives.

Every Christian—no matter their age, sex, or education—is crucial in the battles we face together. A pastor holds a unique position in the operations: his role is not only to fight but to train. Pastors lead and equip the laity for warfare (Eph 4:12–16). Regardless of whether we believe that we are particularly good at our tasks, we remain called and chosen. Yet we clergy don't often have the full picture. There are times when it's clear what our members need, and applying biblical solutions to their lives is pretty straightforward. But there are other times when helping equip people for the idiosyncrasies of their individual spiritual battles that we feel like we're trapped in a pitch-dark room, groping for the light switch. We can't make sense of it all, nor has God asked us to. "For as the heavens are higher than the earth, so are my ways higher than your ways and my thoughts than your thoughts" (Isa 55:9). In short, he is tracking the situation better than we are.

I spent four years as an officer in an army training establishment and school. There, I discovered how military training is intentionally designed to self-perpetuate, ensuring that soldiers, in turn, make soldiers. Soldiers in the military undergo two kinds of training. First, they are trained to serve as warriors. And then, after a few years of experience, they are sent out to train other warriors to do the same. Trainers train trainers indefinitely.

Once you have equipped your people through the service you provide them, they are prepared to do the same for others. Just as angels fight for you, and you fight for your parishioners in ministry contexts, the laity fight for the unbelievers or unchurched with whom they work, live, and play—the people in their ministry contexts. You are priests to them, and they are, in turn, priests to others. And what do priests do? They intercede, and they sacrifice. In the New Testament, Christians are characterized as living sacrifices (Rom 12:1) because they embody Christ's sacrifice. They offer their lives for others in service. They "pray without ceasing" (1 Thess 5:16). Their hearts are stamped with the cross of Jesus. Their minds are governed by his forgiveness and compassion. They are filled with the Holy Spirit. And just as the best soldiers carry battle scars, the souls of Christian priests are shaped by the Lord's wounds. They bear on their bodies "the marks of Jesus" (Gal 6:17). They are, in short, temples of the Holy Spirit. To paraphrase Martin Luther in *The Freedom of a Christian,* "Though they are free from all, they are servants of all." This self-sacrificial attitude of service is manifested daily by Christians within the vast array of their seemingly ordinary vocations. They pray for others, help them in their trials, and perform charitable acts. Their merciful deeds are accompanied by merciful and extraordinary words.

Have you ever observed the way a mother bird feeds her little ones? She finds the worm, brings it back to the nest, and feeds her chicks. Once they grow, they do the same for their own offspring. In a similar way, the laity take what they have received in the church and distribute it to their unbelieving neighbors, with the hope that they will do the same one day. And so, the message continues to penetrate the darkness wherever its beams shine. What parishioners have heard preached by their pastor, they share with the unchurched in their own words.

A tree doesn't produce fruits for its own sake. The church's prayer is that hungry and lost souls, after they "taste and see that the LORD is good" (Ps 34:8), will eventually be drawn to the source of everlasting satisfaction (Matt 5:6). Even when the church looks like an empty ark, surrounded by a dangerous ocean of darkness, appearances are deceiving. God keeps saving sinners. A pastoral goal is equipping the saints: not just for self-service, to protect *themselves*, but to rescue *others* from the darkness in which they sit. Both pastors and people are called to accompany their neighbors through the valley of the shadow of death, freeing *them* from bondage to sin and evil, and welcoming them into the safety of God's kingdom. The topic of spiritual warfare should never limit its application to those who fight. It needs to include those *for whom* we fight. Christ and his angels fight for us, and we in turn for others. In fact, Christ chooses to do so *through* us all, clergy and lay people.

When we believe the threats are real but the mission is possible, a healthy zeal for pastoral ministry is cultivated. Having adopted the eyes of Jesus, observing the world through the lens of angels, we no longer interpret life's experiences and assess our ministry's results as the world would have us do. Instead, Jesus' cross becomes our interpretive hermeneutic. The armor with which we are dressed, though invisible to our eyes, becomes visible by faith. We begin to sense that there is more significance than meets the eye to the intense temptations, unbearable sufferings, and bizarre episodes we've experienced as pastoral caregivers. Fighting on our knees through prayer becomes a gratifying habit instead of an undesirable chore. Reverence toward God's holy processes and the mysteries of faith becomes a natural expression of a virtuous, holistic, and healthy pastoral attitude. We no longer take for granted that we are never alone. We eagerly preside over and attend public worship cognizant of the crowds of heavenly hosts present therein.

Whether blessed to serve as a pastor for a large congregation, remote mission, or small assembly, we

see each of our positions as divinely ordained post-
ings, filled in accordance with the Lord's strategic
vision. Both the glorious victories and the perceived
failures are no longer treated as personal. Instead,
they are attributed to the kingdom of God success-
fully at work despite all satanic resistance. When
we mess up, there is hope. Not one broken thing is
irreparable, just as not one foolish decision is not
forgiven. The kingdom of God, which is *within you*
and *among you* (Luke 17:21), is *bigger* than you. It
includes more than just your ministry and your
people—it includes all saints, of all times and places,
not to mention the angels and archangels.

Spiritual warfare isn't always obvious. It's normally not scary or spooky. It's usually rather mundane. Yet it's always miraculous.

If you could see the hidden battles materialize
before your eyes, you would never skip church,
cut prayers short, or have drifting thoughts when
counseling. Whether you encounter evil in proce-
dural disputes within church committees, doubts
concerning your effectiveness or abilities, deceit-
ful voices in your head, disturbing noises in the
night, or disgraceful feelings in your heart, the
same enemy is hard at work trying to pull you
out of the saving grip of your Savior.

From heaven's perspective, then, all spiritual warfare is serious and real, a matter of life and death. In fact, with all that hinges upon our decisions in these regards, God doesn't leave a lot of those choices up to us but is actively at work behind the scenes. At the very least, he is there with his forgiveness and sovereign wisdom, making right our mistakes and not exposing us to more than we can handle (1 Cor 10:13). Jesus is victor—and in him, so are we. "If God is for us, who can be against us?" (Rom 8:31). The one who conquered our mutual enemies and defeated death by his own death, gives us his word so that they continue to be subdued under the feet of his body, the church. Jesus overcame evil by embracing it on the cross (2 Cor 5:21). He took the darkness upon himself so that we could be filled with his light. What a great exchange! Jesus became a curse in order to break the curse (Gal 3:13). All has been accomplished for us and our salvation.

Although our spiritual enemies are already defeated, they continue to be trampled and subdued by the blood of Jesus. Although we *are* saved, we are still *being* saved. We aren't in heaven yet, though our place there was secured by our Lord when he ascended on high (John 14:3). In the meantime, we fight and battle, suffer and hope, praying and trusting in our Lord's completed and atoning work for us on that first Good Friday. We have guilt and shame to confess, yet we dwell in the forgiveness so richly offered by the baptismal waters and gracious feast of heavenly love. The devil—with his lies, traps, and temptations—may have a lot to say against us, but God gets the final word.

Until we enter heaven or our victorious Lord returns in heavenly glory, the battle continues unceasingly. Otherwise, we would get comfortable and settled in our earthly dwellings. Yet God sends us into the war zone safe and sound, blessed with his presence.

A blessing doesn't just express a hopeful wish but, when it proceeds from the mouth of God, is a word that does exactly what it says. When we hear it and grasp it in faith, we pastors and Christians no longer have any reason to fear the unknown, become demoralized, or feel ill-equipped in our vocations. The words spoken to God's people by our Trinitarian Lord in the Old Testament apply to us still: "The LORD bless you and keep you; the LORD make his face to shine upon you and be gracious to you; the LORD lift up his countenance upon you and give you peace" (Num 6:24–26).

Most gracious, everlasting God, merciful Father,
Thou hast not ordained us unto wrath,
but, that by Thy grace we might be sustained
*   and blessed.*
Therefore, we do heartily beseech Thee,
*   dear Lord and God,*
support us throughout our whole lives
and give charge to Thy holy angels,
who serve before Thy face continually,
that they watch over and care for us,
to defend us in body and soul against the craft
*   of the devil and his angels;*
that we abide with Thee unto the end;
through Thy beloved Son, Jesus Christ,
our Lord and Saviour.
Amen.

—Wilhelm Loehe, *Seed Grains of Prayer,* p. 408

Resources

> *Rites and Resources for Pastoral Care.*
> Lutheran Church of Australia, 1998.

This resource has been one of my own personal favorites. When asked to visit families undergoing unique challenges to their faith—recovering from abortion, breakdown of marriage, suicidal tendencies—I always carry this little book with me. The resources are short and clear. They offer practical instruction and guidelines on their immediate use and aftercare for the one suffering or struggling. The section on "Spiritual Oppression" provides some classic short rites of exorcism, that are grounded in biblical quotes and coupled with ancient prayers. The rites pertaining to the blessing of persons and places or objects are centered in Christ Jesus and the work of the Holy Trinity in Christian lives, safeguarding hearers from any temptation toward superstition. I continue to use the order for house blessing because the Scriptures and prayers are short yet theologically profound.

➣ *Lutheran Service Book: Pastoral Care Companion.* Concordia, 2007.

The "Resources for Pastoral Care" section of *The Lutheran Service Book: Pastoral Care Companion* is a must-have for pastors of all denominations in offering spiritual care to their parishioners in the midst of the vast array of family and personal struggles that they endure. Whether addressing those struggling with grief and bereavement, ethical and moral crises, or issues of demonic entry points or demonic involvement—of a sexual nature, mental disorders, and unhealthy psychological states—the carefully selected Scriptures and tailored prayers are sure to equip the pastor and people for spiritual battle. "Times of Spiritual Distress" includes a section of resources dealing with "Occult Practices and Demonic Affliction." However, the material on this subject is too generic and limited, and would not likely suffice in the case of an actual encounter with demonic possession or even oppression. The *Rites and Resources* mentioned above is much more useful in that regard.

> ⮞ Ashcraft, Jack. *The Ancient Orthodox Ritual of Exorcism*. Ashcraft, 2011.

Many pastors are hesitant to use rituals in exorcism. We should rightly be cautious and avoid all sorts of superstition or ceremonies that pivot around the man who performs them. But when flowing from faith and humility and accompanied by sincere prayer and trust in God, some rituals are helpful consisting of ancient prayers and direct quotations from the Holy Scriptures. After all, an exorcism is really just speaking the very words of the Holy Scriptures, reminding everybody present, including the devil, to whom they belong and who is in charge. I prefer this Orthodox version, over the *Roman Ritual*, because it is shorter, and easier to use. Putting aside the few scattered prayers to angels and saints, any Protestant clergy can feel comfortable with the material. Rituals such as this one, when used properly, can be an effective part of the ministry of deliverance.

> Bonhoeffer, Dietrich. *Life Together.* HarperOne, 2009.

The spiritual battle never consists of just you. It involves a whole community of believers. Dietrich Bonhoeffer, philosopher, professor, pastor, and modern martyr, was renowned for the agonizing ethical dilemmas he confronted in the face of evil forces. Bonhoeffer was not only familiar with the evils of society and the sin in the hearts of others, but he was also quick to confess the darkness that abounded within his own heart. Consequently, there is no such thing as an ideal society or perfect community. Yet our "life together" is not only bearable but beautiful when we let the forgiveness of sins govern our ways and attitudes. After all, as St. Augustine put it, the community of the Holy Trinity in heaven is reflected in Christian communities on earth. Love, then is the heart of the church, though it's a heart that remains broken and sinful. By taking principles intuitive to fraternal communities and applying them to congregational life, this book can serve as a guide for fostering and developing a Christian spirit within small groups and even families. Bonhoeffer offers many practical tips, that are couched in deep

theological and sacramental language, and supported with personal examples that resonate with
any Christian, equipping readers with an attitude
of Christian love and service.

> Danielou, Jean. *The Angels and Their
>   Mission.* The Newman Press, Westminister,
>   1957.

Father Jean Danielou, a Jesuit priest and educa-
tor, offers a comprehensive discussion on the subject of both good and bad angels, based on the
Scriptures and patristics. Some of his perspectives
and insights are not to be found in other books on
angelology, especially since Danielou boldly tack-
les some difficult Bible passages that remain relatively untouched by others. Due to his reliance on
the church fathers and other early sources such as
Pseudo-Dionysius, sometimes his assertions can
be mistaken for gospel truth. But astute biblical
scholars and pastors who can navigate through
some of those controversial elements will discover
a wealth of knowledge and stimulating commentary on the history, work, and community of angels.
They will also find themselves rejoicing in all of
God's great gifts to humankind.

> Gerhard, Johann. *Meditations on Divine Mercy.* Concordia, 2003.

One of my favorite prayer books by a Lutheran father of the faith, *Meditations on Divine Mercy* is infused with lovely poetic, theological, and Scripturally based petitions of repentance and, as the title suggests, appeals to God's divine mercy. And God is glad to offer it in Jesus Christ. I have included this prayer book as an effective spiritual weapon in fighting the devil and temptation. Each prayer is implicitly penitential, keeping the soul humble. Historic prayers stand the test of time precisely because they so effectively express the timeless cries of the human heart and condition, the Lord's Prayer being the chief of them all. Praying the petitions in this book is sure to help protect you from any pastoral arrogance and circumvent any thinking that successful ministry is about the results you see or experiences you feel. Instead, they reinforce the notion that all Christian fruits flourish from the tree of Christ's cross.

> Hallesby, Ole. *Prayer*. Augsburg Fortress, 1994.

A wonderful, easy-to-read, classic book on prayer written by one of Norway's leading Christian teachers and devotional writers. Hallesby played a leading role in the church's opposition to the Nazis and was confined to a concentration camp for two years. Those who have suffered much are often the best writers and preachers. His writings are rich in truth and maturity. Although he emphasizes faith in God's grace as pivotal to a healthy prayer life and spiritual warfare, he can sound legalistic at a first read. However, when one appreciates the mystical character of prayer, which is impossible to accurately express in words, Hallesby's understanding of prayer becomes an expression of the sanctified life. Former concerns are overshadowed by the reality that God—not man—is the main player, worker, and mover within all Christian disciplines.

views the nature and function of faith. Koenig's book is rather refreshing in an intellectual culture that has often been critical of religion as a tool for healing. It also serves as a useful reference for unbelievers who negate the importance of faith, spirituality, and religion for holistic health.

> Lewis, C. S. *The Great Divorce*. HarperCollins, 2015.

Who would have thought that a tale about a bunch of human residents of hell taking a bus trip to heaven would have become a Christian cult classic? A unique and imaginative tale, it is the most thought-provoking piece of literature on the nature of heaven and hell. Readers become convinced that the lonely, dark bitter lives of the damned of hell reside where they truly belong. They wouldn't be any happier elsewhere. They wouldn't enjoy heaven. These curious tourists give it a try. But the music, crowds, light, and heavenly party atmosphere of it all is so diametrically opposed to what they have grown accustomed to that they absolutely hate it and eagerly await the ride home to Hades. In pastoral ministry, apologetics and evangelism, I have found this little book to be an indispensable tool in helping resolve the issue of a loving God sending people to hell as punishment. Lewis has us conceptualize hell, not only as a place, but also as a state of being. Hell is portrayed as a personal condition. Lewis does a brilliant job at robbing hell of its dazzling mystique, and presents it as an existentially meaningless place filled with lonely people. Although this book won't convert unbelieving readers to Christianity, it will open their eyes to the undesirability of an afterlife without the presence of God.

> Lewis, C. S. *The Screwtape Letters.* Time Incorporated, 1961.

There's good reason why this is C. S. Lewis' most popular work of fiction outside of The Chronicles of Narnia. It is definitely the best exposition of the reasoning and strategies the devil uses to draw people away from the kingdom of God. This book consists of a series of letters written between two demons in the unholy army, discussing tactics to destroy a certain Christian enemy. To their dismay, by the grace of God, they fail. Highly entertaining, intelligent, and comical, *The Screwtape Letters* reveal Lewis' genius regarding the human psyche and its relationship to spirituality. It is no wonder churches have used this as a book study for youth groups and adult studies on the topic of spiritual warfare. It's a mighty weapon for parishioners who know their Bibles, desire to grow in Christian virtue and faith, and appreciate wholesome British writing.

> Neuhaus, Richard John. *Death On a Friday Afternoon: Meditations on the Last Words of Jesus from the Cross.* Basic Books, 2000.

This is one of my favorite reads in keeping my eyes fixed upon Jesus, the author and perfector of our faith. Catholic theologian and pastor Neuhaus convinces the reader of the benefits of refusing to race too quickly through Lent to Easter. His profound insights regarding the daily impact and necessity of reflecting upon the crucifixion of Christ are conveyed by his accessible writing style—seasoned with intriguing personal anecdotes. Since the greatest offense to the devil is the cross of Calvary, meditating continually upon Christ's words and work on Good Friday is sure to prove to be one of the most effective weapons against our evil foe. Protestants will find some segments of this short book disagreeable theologically, but the pros heavily outweigh any potential cons in this ecumenical and mature devotional.

> Nouwen, Henri. *The Return of the Prodigal Son*. Doubleday, 1992.

Having worked extensivly with mentally and physically challenged adults in inner-city Toronto, Ontario, Canada, Father Nouwen is full of wisdom, humility, and compassion. Most of his books are devotional in nature. They seek ways of communicating the healing love of Jesus to broken people. While unpacking the painting by Renaissance artist Rembrandt, *The Return of the Prodigal Son*, Nouwen reverently and poetically guides the reader through the topic of forgiveness. He explores the ways in which we are forgiven and need to forgive by comparing us to each of the characters in Jesus' parable. The parallels that he draws are relevant and sagacious due to his deep appreciation for the complexities of the human mind and soul, including idolatrous obstacles in accepting and showing mercy. I have some difficulty endorsing his chapter on "forgiving God"—applicable to victims of abuse who are angry with God for his apparent indifference to their tragic circumstances—though the author admits the controversy and does his best to qualify the idea. Overall it's a wonderful book for sharpening pastoral care skill and shaping the pastoral heart.

➢ Postman, Neil. *Amusing Ourselves to Death.*
   Penguin, 1985.

Some may find this book to be an unusual resource
for spiritual warfare—especially given the fact that
the author is an agnostic. However, Christians
have a lot to learn from Postman's brilliant critical approach to media and popular culture. He
includes a priceless chapter on the impact of secular culture on the way Christians worship. His
argument is that Christians are their own worst
enemies when they uncritically import technolo-
gies into the life of their churches. It inadvertently
robs our worship—which is also an expression
of our doctrine—of its sacred and holy character. After all, our behavior is shaped by our beliefs.
Postman implies that Christian worship deserves a
fitting, reverent environment with lots of room for
mystery. The spiritual battles that happen during
public worship are unique, which is why every
Christian should take Postman's warnings and cul-
tural commentary seriously. Other authors have
made similar points, but Postman does it in the
most entertaining and—shall we say—amusing way.

> Ristau, Harold. *My First Exorcism: What the Devil Taught a Lutheran Pastor about Counter-Cultural Spirituality.* Wipf & Stock, 2016.

The topic presumes a certain level of spiritual and intellectual maturity, and is not intended for skeptics or those who frighten easily. I dare to say that it is one of the only books of its kind because it delves into subject matter that many demonologists avoid, asking the toughest of questions without offering pat answers. I share my experience as a pastor. Although intended primarily for pastors, lay people will be fascinated to get a window into this unique dimension of ministry. My personal experiences specifically pertaining to demon possession act as a springboard for addressing the general idiosyncrasies of spiritual warfare in a North American context. Because I have so candidly shared my failures and fears, pastors of all denominations—who are having difficulties carrying their crosses in their respective ministries—have found these reflections to be an inspiring source of comfort and hope. Although it is specifically about spiritual warfare, the underlying message is one that centers upon living in the knowledge of God's love in Christ, even when we feel ourselves surrounded by thick and abnormal clouds of darkness that don't seem to recede as fast as we wish.

Epigraph Sources

Notes

1. St. Chrysostom, *Homilies on Hebrews*, Homily XIV (Heb 8:1–2), *Nicene and Post-Nicene Fathers of the Christian Church*, ed. Philip Schaff (T&T Clark; Eerdmans, 1889), 14:438.

2. Philipp Melanchthon, "Lord God, to Thee We Give All Praise," *Lutheran Service Book* (Concordia, 2006), no. 522, v. 3.

3. St. Chrysostom, *Homilies on Hebrews*, Homily III (Heb 1:6–8), *Nicene and Post-Nicene Fathers*, 14:377.

4. The collect for Michaelmas can be found in various prayer books; see, for example, *Lutheran Service Book: Pastoral Care Companion* (Concordia, 2007), 612, or *The 1662 Book of Common Prayer: International Edition*, eds. Samuel L. Bray and Drew Nathaniel Keane (IVP Academic, 2021), 232.

5. "The Litany," see *Book of Common Prayer* 1662 (IVP Academic, 2021), 34; see also *Book of Common Prayer* 2019, 95.

6. Johann Gerhard, *The Sermon and the Propers*, translated by Fred G. Lindemann, vol. 4 (Concordia, 1959), 72, 74–75.

7. History is littered with the reality of human sacrifices to demons, whether ritualistically among the Mayans and Aztecs or politically among kamikaze pilots or the Islamic Jihad. "They sacrificed their sons and their daughters to the demons" (Ps 106:37). Yet even those who know service to the devil is bad and want freedom may not count the cost. In my own personal experience with the ministry of deliverance, I have found that many who are physically oppressed or possessed by demons seek the aid of Christ out of personal desperation in this life. They want to be free from the devil but don't want to belong to God. But that option does not exist. For good or for ill we all belong to somebody, and worldly freedom from everybody and everything is actually more like hell than heaven. Some seek freedom via suicide, others seek freedom by avoiding their brothers and sisters in Christ. There are worse things than possession. I would rather that a sinner be plagued by one thousand demons throughout the week and find him seeking God's grace and mercy at the altar of Christ during the Sunday morning worship than be entirely delivered and healed from his oppression, never to step foot into the Lord's church again. Not one of us is better off restored from our ailments if our healing results in a less active spiritual life with

Christ, as we find him incarnate among us in Christian worship.

8. St. Athanasius, Letter VI, 9, 11, Easter 335, 523.

9. First sphere: 1. Seraphim, 2. Cherubim, 3. Thrones. Second sphere: 4. Dominations (also translated as Lordships), 5. Virtues (also translated as Powers), 6. Powers (also translated as Authorities). Third sphere: 7. Principalities, 8. Archangels, 9. Angels.

10. Joseph the Hymnographer, "Stars of the Morning so Gloriously Bright," *Lutheran Service Book* (Concordia, 2006), no. 520, v. 4.

11. The oppressed fluctuate within the range of their abilities to control their human faculties—the least noticeable being a consistent disinterest in spiritual affairs involving Christ, the most serious being blackouts or zombie-like moments where the individual simply stares aloof, often with darkened eyes, having no recollection of the moment.

12. Benjamin T. G. Mayes, "Research Notes: Demon Possession and Exorcism in Lutheran Orthodoxy," *Concordia Theological Quarterly* 81, nos. 3–4 (2017): 331–36, here 332–34.

13. Eyewitnessing less offensive but still unnatural abilities such as knowledge of secret things, or the ability to predict the future, are also clear reasons for grave concern. I have written a book entitled *My First Exorcism* (Wipf and Stock,

2016) for those who would like to explore the subject in more depth.

14. See John W. Kleinig, *Grace upon Grace: Spirituality for Today* (Concordia, 2008), 244–48.

15. C. F. W. Walther, *God Grant It*, trans. Gerhard Grabenhofer (Concordia Publishing House, 2006), 838–39.

16. St. Chrysostom, *Homilies on Hebrews*, Homily III (Heb 1:6–8), *Nicene and Post-Nicene Fathers*, 14:377.

17. Martin Luther, *Small Catechism* (1529), explanation of article two of the Apostles' Creed (see *Lutheran Service Book*, 322–23).

18. This was a traditional opening sentence of the baptismal rite. See, for example, Martin Luther, *The Order for Baptism* (1523) and *The Order for Baptism Newly Revised* (1526), *Luther's Works [American Edition]*. 82 vols. projected. (Concordia; Fortress, 1955–1986, 2009–), 53:96, 107.

19. Dietrich Bonhoeffer, *No Rusty Swords*, trans. and ed. Edwin H. Robertson (Harper & Row, 1965).

20. Andrew T. Lincoln, *Ephesians*, Word Biblical Commentary, 42 (Nelson, 1990), 449.

21. Fyodor Dostoevsky, *Brothers Karamazov*, "The Grand Inquisitor," book V, chapter 5.

22. I write more about her story in my book, *My First Exorcism*.

23. A few include the following: The binding of
    Isaac and the offering of a goat acts as a type
    of Christ's binding on the cross in our stead
    (Gen 22:1–18). The Passover in Egypt by the
    angel of death recalls the rescue of Christian
    people, resting securely behind the blood-
    stained doorposts of their hearts (Exod 12:1–24).
    Jonah's bursting out from the belly of the whale
    prophesizes the resurrection of Christ from
    the tomb and his victory over the grave (Jonah
    1:1–4:11). Joshua's entrance into the promised
    land (Josh 1:1–9), and Ezekiel's vision of rebirth
    in the valley of dry bones (Ezek 37:1–14) are also
    types of Jesus' resurrection and the deliverance
    that he brings. (From The Church of England's
    Common Worship). See also the "Vigil of Easter"
    in *Lutheran Service Book: Altar Book*, 529–51.

24. See John W. Kleinig's outstanding book *Grace
    upon Grace: Spirituality for Today* (Concordia,
    2008). Kleinig does a remarkable job unpacking
    the paradox of Christian spirituality. He
    demonstrates how a Christian's spiritual growth
    and strength are hidden phenomena. Spiritual
    advancement doesn't occur by our efforts and
    can't be grasped by our senses. Instead, it occurs
    uniquely in the cross of our Lord and Savior,
    experienced by faith as belief.

25. *Lutheran Service Book* (Concordia, 2006), 254.

26. Harold L. Senkbeil, *The Care of Souls: Cultivating a Pastor's Heart* (Lexham Press, 2019), 137.

27. This is well expressed in a scene in C. S. Lewis's science fiction novel *Perelandra*, when the aliens stand in awe when first meeting a human, because he belonged to the race of which the Creator of all creatures had deigned to become.

28. Consider the respect a soldier shows toward a loaded weapon. He feels both admiration and trepidation for its capabilities. At war, even the winning side, surrounded by their own armies, still feels fear. As a military chaplain maneuvering amidst the powerfully outfitted gunmen, I would find my heart pounding in deep appreciation and respect for their powerful size and force. How dwarfed, vulnerable, and insignificant I felt many times—filled with awe, surrounded by the mighty presence of infantrymen. And yet these earthly armies are but a tiny shadow of the invisible angelic ones. We will fall on our faces in heaven when we see our Lord, surrounded by the heavenly hosts.

29. Clement of Rome, 1 Clement 34; *Treasury of Daily Prayer* (Concordia, 2008), 1477.

30. Many versions of this ancient service exist today. My personal favorite is found in the *Lutheran Service Book* (Concordia, 2006), 253–59. The Church of England's *Book of Common Prayer* also

includes a version (Church Publishing, 1979, 127–35; Anglican Liturgy Press, 2019, 57–67).

31. See C. S. Lewis, *The Great Divorce* (HarperCollins, 2015) for an entertaining and philosophically insightful fictional commentary on the nature of hell. A bunch of human residents of hell take a bus trip to heaven only to discover that it is an impossible fit. Lewis demonstrates how the lonely, dark, bitter lives of the damned of hell reside where they truly belong and wouldn't be any happier elsewhere. Hell, as the absence of God, is both a place and a state of being. Hell becomes the natural resting place of those who reject heaven. It is both heaven's alternative and the ultimate expression of human freedom—freedom from God's love.

32. From the "Kyrie" in the Divine Service, see, for example, *Lutheran Service Book*, 152–53. This petition is also used in the "Litany for Evening Prayer," see *Lutheran Service Book*, 250.

33. Martin Buber, *Ten Rungs: Collected Hassidic Sayings*, 2nd edition (Routledge, 2002), 85.